The Tinderbox Way

Mark Bernstein

ISBN: 1-8845-1146-5

Eastgate Systems, Inc. 134 Main Street, Watertown MA 02472 USA

info@eastgate.com   http://www.eastgate.com

The Tinderbox Way

1. Introduction: The Tinderbox Way

Tinderbox is a software tool for making, analyzing, and sharing notes. It's an unusual piece of software. At a time when most new programs are updates and revisions within a familiar genre, Tinderbox attempts something new.

Tinderbox is a **personal content management assistant**, a tool for notes. Notes are intensely personal, but their impact on your effectiveness and accomplishment, public and private, can be tremendous. Writing things down, in a place where we can find them again, helps us make sure that we can consider every aspect of our decisions. The importance of making, analyzing, and sharing notes applies not merely to weighty decisions, like choosing what kind of car to buy or in which mutual fund to invest, but also to the hundreds of tiny decisions we make every day, selecting what we'll do next and what we'll postpone.

I often hear people talk about a book, a film, a party that changed their lives. But how many people have heard about a book that might have been, for them, *that* crucial book, only to forget all about it? How often do we fail to find the time to see a film or a play we ought to have seen? How many times have we been too busy or preoccupied to remember to drop by a party where we just might have met someone who would have changed... *everything?*

Our choices are important, and intensely personal. If we make them by drifting, if we leave them to chance and memory, how can we be confident that we are doing all we can do? And doing what we ought? We learn by remembering, by reviewing experiences. By preserving our notes, we can create new opportunities for learning. What were you reading, this time last year? What do you think about it today? What do you think, now, about that movie that seemed so original, or so controversial, just a few months ago? Will you even remember it, a few months from now? Who will remind you?

An Energetic Assistant

Tinderbox is designed to help you write things down, find them, think about them, and share them. Tinderbox is an **assistant**. It's meant to help, to facilitate. It's not a methodology or a code. It's a way to write things down, link them up, and share them. It's a chisel, guided by your hand and your intelligence.

Tinderbox is personal in another sense, as well; unlike most corporate software today, Tinderbox was designed and implemented by a person – not by a committee, a corporation, or a focus group. That person is me: Mark Bernstein. I designed Tinderbox, and wrote just about every line of the tens of thousands of lines that make Tinderbox run. Tinderbox is the product of an individual vision. It wasn't written to meet requirements or specs or to adhere to business rules. Along the way, there have been thousands of decisions — engineering decisions, artistic decisions, operational decisions. In the end, I made the choices.

I didn't need to persuade the Development department to code Tinderbox the way I wanted: I was the development team. I didn't have to fight Management and Marketing for features. They work for me. But Tinderbox has always been short of resources: never enough time, never enough hands to do all the work. I made plenty of mistakes, and when those mistakes became visible, I had to decide whether to live with them or to start over.

According to current wisdom, this is the wrong way to build software. We're told that software specifications should be based on meticulous studies of user needs and corporate goals, that specialized interaction designers should plan the interactions and specialized graphic designers should plan the graphics, that the code needs to be planned and specified by product specialists and then written and tested in software factories located in distant, low-wage lands. Documentation, packaging, and marketing specialists add their special skills.

Good software sometimes comes from organizations like this, but it's a process of consensus, of design by negotiation. At its worst extreme – an extreme we see more and more often in software today – it generates the blandness of design by committee.

When Apple announced the original iMac, our designer asked, "Why would anyone want a VT100 made out of colored plastic on their desk?" Here at Eastgate, we'd predicted a very different product and expected the new machine would prove a debacle. We were completely wrong. A few weeks later, I spent a day visiting art galleries on Santa Fe's Canyon Road, and the most prosperous galleries all had colorful new iMacs atop their stylish desks. Some of those desks were 17th-century hand-carved Spanish heirlooms, some were spectacular steel-and-wood fantasies of contemporary crafts, but on all of them stood Bondi Blue iMacs shaped just like that long-obsolete dumb terminal.

The galleries weren't responding to the retro tech allusion: they responded to the iMac because it was different. It was designed. Someone had thought about it – it wasn't just another beige box. It didn't matter that the old beige box might have been better, in some ways; the iMac was trying to do what the old package didn't, and you could sense a personality and a vision behind that attempt.

A Personal Content Management Assistant

Tinderbox is *personal*. It's designed to help you do your work better and to enjoy it more. It does this by helping to manage *notes*, by which I mean all sorts of specific, meaningful information. It helps you to make notes, to analyze them, and to share them with colleagues, customers, and friends. We call this overall process of making, analyzing, and sharing information *content management*.

Finally, and crucially, Tinderbox is an *assistant*. It does not impose a way of working; it's neither a workflow or a methodology. Tinderbox doesn't tell you how to take notes, but instead provides you with a number of different ways of making them. Tinderbox doesn't suggest an optimal way to share information, but instead offers a variety of ways in which you might share information, in forms that your collaborators will find convenient and useful.

The Productivity Puzzle

If Tinderbox is an *assistant*, it should help you. Do our computers actually help? Or do they merely replace some old-fashioned clerical drudgery – ledger books and file cabinets – with new chores like reading spam and filling out Web forms? Economists, looking to measure the productivity gains realized by widespread adoption of personal computers in business, have found it surprisingly difficult to demonstrate that computers help at all.

I'd like to suggest that this isn't the fault of the computers. It's not a matter of bad design, of poor user interfaces or faulty error messages or cryptic documentation. Computers *have* given us enormous wealth and productivity, but we've chosen to spend that wealth in a way that makes it hard to see and to measure.

Computers in my childhood were exotic, romantic, expensive things. Today, they are ubiquitous in the workplace, in schools, in homes. When we watch movies about business life set in the quite-recent past – Jack Lemmon's office in *The Apartment,* say – we marvel at the clumsiness of business procedures that were, quite recently, state of the art. Banking transactions that once were manually recorded by tellers and checked by clerks are now handled by robotic ATMs or rendered unnecessary by credit cards. Mechanical phone indexes, rotary dialers, electric typewriters: all seem as arcane today as the crimson-colored ribbons, called "red tape", that tied bundles of documents together in an era before manila folders and paper clips had been invented. Cutting and pasting were, only yesterday, performed with glue, and a misspelled word was best repaired by retyping the page on which it appeared. Computers, obviously, save time. They make us greatly more productive (and much less bored) at work.

Yet, if you examine economic statistics, it's remarkably hard to show that computers have improved everyday business productivity [11]. It takes about as much time, and about as much expense, to compose routine business correspondence today as it did a generation ago. The costs of making a sales call or closing a real-estate transaction, measured in real dollars, are roughly what they used to be. A new best-selling novel costs about as much as an entrée in a nice restaurant – just as it did in 1930, and in 1790. But that book in 1930 was written on a manual typewriter and set in hot type; the 18th-century book was written in longhand with a quill pen and hand-set by skilled compositors who picked tiny letters out of type trays. Today, the writer uses a word processor and delivers electronic files to the publisher, and the publisher in turn sends electronic files to the printer. Yet, somehow, economists cannot detect a increase in productivity.

Where did the money go? Computers do enhance our productivity; we simply have spent that productivity in ways that are not always, immediately, apparent.

- Business materials today are more attractive, more accurate, and better designed. I can remember, as late as 1980, receiving an annual report for a publicly traded corporation that had been prepared on a typewriter and reproduced by mimeograph. Today, the most routine business correspondence is typeset, and we think nothing of adding line drawings and illustrations to print collateral, even when the material is designed for a very small audience. Even where the audience is a single manager, we may exploit graphic design tools that, in the past, would have been far out of reach
- The 1990s witnessed a presentation arms race in the lecture hall and in the conference room. People who once thought it sufficient to use chalk on slate now routinely create elaborate PowerPoint® presentations. Firms that once answered technical queries from other businesses with plain typed reports – the original "white papers" – now respond with print-on-demand books, custom-generated full-color reports, and elaborate Web sites.

- We replaced a legion of boring jobs with vastly more interesting, autonomous, and fulfilling positions. Just after World War II, my mother won a competition for a magazine intern position and arrived, by train, in Manhattan, where she joined the staff of a fashion magazine. Her manager was a woman — a remarkable circumstance, even though the manager's father was a movie star. Early on, she gave my mother crucial advice: "Patsy," she said, "never let them know you can type." Because she was thought to be incapable of typing and filing, my mother got the opportunity to be a newspaperwoman.
- As late as 1990, a keynote speaker at an international computer conference could assert with confidence that personal computers would not be accepted in the executive suite until we could get rid of keyboards. Keyboards were for secretaries and file clerks. Yesterday's secretaries and file clerks became today's branch managers, software designers, and IT directors. They make a lot more money and consume a lot of expensive resources in their new roles – and thus seem less productive. But that's just a statistical illusion.
- Each elevator once required a full-time operator. This must have been a terribly dull job, moving up and down, day after day. Easily automated jobs are unsuitable for people; as a society, we've chosen to spend some of our productivity gains in order to avoid assigning people to dull, dirty, and dangerous work.

When a business makes a profit, it may choose to spend some of that profit making the workplace more pleasant – painting the walls, buying more comfortable chairs, or throwing a spectacular holiday party. Some of these may be profit-earning investments, but others are simply profit sharing: a business rewards its workers through both monetary and non-monetary rewards. As a society, we've chosen to use the profits that computer productivity has generated on non-monetary rewards.

Some of those choices now seem wise, and we wonder why we waited so long. Others strike me as less convincing, especially the shift toward elaborate production in internal communication and presentations. But, if our rival is sending typeset and illustrated proposals to the Boss, dare we limit ourselves to the economical simplicity of plain white sheets and hand-lettered sketches?

In any case, that's where the money went. Society made its collective choice. The computer did its share, and if we have spent the profits unwisely or imprudently, it's wrong to blame the computer that generated the opportunity in the first place.

The Right Way To Do It

In over twenty years of designing and building hypertext tools at Eastgate, we've been very reluctant to tell people what to do, to presume to instruct the people who use our software. Our opinions, such as they are, are embodied in the design.

This book, then, is a radical departure from our customs. I'm not writing in the confident assurance that I know the best way to use a tool like Tinderbox. Often, I know several ways to do something, but not which way is best. Often, I know several things worth doing, but not which one is worth doing first. And, experience has shown time and again that, when I believe I do know best, I may very well be wrong.

Software designers, like all artists, work to anticipate the needs of their audience, but one of the first lessons of software design is that real people use real software in really astonishing ways. *The street finds its use for things,* as William Gibson wrote in *Neuromancer.*

But Tinderbox is a very new kind of software, and even computer professionals have grown unaccustomed to truly new software. People ask me, over and over, *What should I do?* I receive letters and email from all over the world, asking, *Where do I start?* And, *What do I need to learn?* This book contains my best advice.

Throughout this book, I affect more confidence in my opinions and in my conclusions than is actually warranted. Often, experience and evidence weigh on both sides of a question. If I properly qualified each bold assertion, this book would be long, tiresome, and tentative.

If you see a better way to do something about which this book is silent, you may well be right. If you envision a new application we don't mention, it may well prove superior to the examples discussed here. If you find that your experience does not agree with mine, your working environment may well be different. These are the notes of an early explorer; I hope you will find them a trustworthy guide but, if you find the map disagrees with the terrain before you, by all means trust the terrain.

Learning about Tinderbox

This book assumes that you are generally familiar with the elements of Tinderbox. If you're new to Tinderbox, it may help if you explore the program a little, and spend some time with the manual, just to get your bearings.

Tinderbox is actively growing, and Eastgate is constantly adding improvements and new features. We recommend using the latest release of the program – even if it happens to be newer than the Tinderbox used in these pages. The confusion created by small discrepancies in the program's appearance will be offset by better performance in the latest version. You can always find the latest release at

http://www.eastgate.com/Tinderbox/

Since Tinderbox comes with a year of free upgrades, you'll most likely be able to download the latest version and get down to work immediately.

Remember to try things out. Tinderbox makes it so easy to build large and complicated projects that, at times, the project may outrun your understanding. If you aren't quite sure how a feature works, try making a sample document just for practice. Many of the Hands-On projects described in this book make excellent practice documents;

most take only a few minutes to build once you've grasped the underlying concepts.

Things Change

This book was written during development of Tinderbox for Macintosh versions 2 and 3 and Tinderbox for Windows 1.0.

Over time, Tinderbox will grow and change. We'll adapt this book as well, but some aspects of the program – especially cosmetic aspects – might not coincide exactly with the descriptions here. You'll find complete, up-to-date information in the *Tinderbox User's Manual* and in the *Tinderbox Release Notes*.

The *User's Manual* is your best resource for understanding the mechanics of Tinderbox. Here, we'll concentrate on bigger questions and fundamental concepts.

About the scenarios

The scenarios and examples in this book are based on real cases, but the details are entirely imaginary. Any resemblance to actual persons living or dead, places, or organizations is entirely coincidental.

Acknowledgements

My colleagues at Eastgate, and in the hypertext research community, played large and crucial roles. At Eastgate, Eric Cohen and Diane Greco supplied dozens of ideas and plenty of useful skepticism when things started to go astray. Eric was the original Tinderbox tech writer and tester, burdens more recently shouldered by Jen Muehlbauer. Meryl R. Cohen, Barbara Bean, and Elin Sjursen lent willing hands to tackle what needed to be done. Robina Williams provided invaluable editorial advice. Tinderbox takes many fine ideas from *Storyspace*, the hypertext writing environment originally written by Jay David Bolter, Michael Joyce, and John B. Smith, and from *VIKI*, the pioneering spatial hypertext system created by Catherine C.

Marshall and Frank Shipman. The good parts of Tinderbox are
largely theirs.

2. Notes

Taking Note

What are notes? Observations. Lists. Ideas. Dreams.

Notes are what we write when we are writing to ourselves. We might share some notes with others – most often with our assistants, colleagues, confidants, with people who help us get things done. The primary audience of a note is almost always our future self.

We might intend to use some notes to advance a different kind of writing project: to write a book or an article, a policy proposal or a school paper. We might suppose that, someday, our grandchildren might read our notes and learn something about us that they won't find in family photographs or from our more formal accomplishments. But this, too, is secondary. We treasure the notebooks and travel journals of our ancestors because they wrote them for themselves, not for us – because in their notes, we hear them speaking to themselves in their everyday voices.

> **Tip**: Give thought to preserving notes long after their immediate purpose might be fulfilled. Storage is cheap, and will become less and less expensive every year. You never know what you might want someday, and you have no idea whatsoever what your great-grandchildren might want.
>
> For example, consider notes that you make in order to remind yourself to do something. You may be tempted, once you've finished the task, to delete the note. Don't! Instead, keep a container that holds a list of tasks you've finished. If the container is someday filled with old tasks, just copy the container and paste it into an archive document.

In the same vein, it's a great idea to make notes whenever you can, about whatever you see. However superb your memory, you won't remember everything. Knowing you've written something down, you'll have one less thing to worry about. And, once you trust yourself to make and keep notes, you'll be able to rely more on your notemaking system and will not need worry so much about what you might forget.

Storage Is Free

It might seem wasteful to store notes you don't expect to need again. Those old notes, after all, take up disk space. Disks fill up, and we're accustomed to thinking of storage as expensive.

This conclusion is wrong. Tinderbox notes are so compact that you can store them forever. This seems hard to believe: let's run the numbers.

As I write this, a top-of-the-line hard disk will hold about 1000 Gb of information and will cost about $1000. It's likely to last a long time, but let's be conservative and expect to replace it after three years. A fairly long note from our ToDo list – a grocery list, perhaps – might run a few hundred words, and Tinderbox itself records metadata: the time the note was first made, the identity of its author. So this note might take about 1K of space on disk. Saving that 1K for three years will cost about one millionth of a dollar.

Three years from now, we'll replace the disk drive. Thanks to Moore's Law, the new drive will most likely cost about 1/4 of what we originally paid. But, even if the price of storage never decreases, we can continue buying new drives for millennia before the cost of storing this note will buy a cup of coffee.

The value of the time you spend deciding to delete a note in order to conserve space will exceed by many orders of magnitude the cost of saving that note indefinitely.

> **Tip**: From time to time, you *will* want to declutter your workspaces and notebooks. Old notes might be useful someday, but you don't need to look at them all the time. So, periodically, plan to move obsolete notes and stale tasks to archival spaces. But don't waste time wondering if things are worth

keeping: in cyberspace, our attics have become so
big that the cost of an extra note – or an extra
million notes – is negligible.

Design Note: Getting It Down

Two assurances are central to the Tinderbox approach. Writing a
note must be fast, and the note, once written, must be stored reliably.
Speed and safety are each essential.

Swift notemaking depends on making the "new note" gesture simple.
Some early programs, like the brilliant NoteCards [8], began by
asking users to classify and categorize each note, even before it was
written. That turned out poorly; until you've written a note, it's hard
to know exactly where it fits. In practice, if you ask people for lots of
metadata about their notes before the note is written, you'll get lots of
hurried and imprecise answers. Writers will know that they can't rely
on their own hastily-scrawled metadata, and won't be able rely on it
or use it.

Tinderbox makes notes quickly. Press **return**, and you can begin
typing the title. Press **return** again, and you're all set. Some metadata
– the time when the note was created, the person who made it – are
set automatically. (You can often arrange for Tinderbox to
automatically add additional metadata as well.)

Tinderbox's prototypes (Chapter 4) encourage you to build better-
structured documents. By choosing a prototype, you can save typing
and set lots of attributes with a single gesture; prototypes provide an
immediate reward for taking a moment to think about the document
structure. At the same time, Tinderbox agents (Chapter 7) can scan
your document continuously, seeking to find patterns and to discover
structure.

Because notes are so personal and so important – and because, even
with Tinderbox, they represent so much time and work – it is vital to
feel confident your work is safe. Everyone agrees that programs
should never lose data or create unreadable files. That's easy to say,
but nobody today can deliver on the promise. Even spaceflight-

qualified software, subjected to years of careful testing and planned to bear the load of billion-dollar missions, sometimes fails.

Tinderbox files are XML; XML turned out to be a crucial element in the assuring that you will always have access to your information. XML is simple and standard, so a host of software tools can work with it. Second, XML files are repairable; isolated errors can be identified and fixed. Finally, XML files are designed so that people can read them. Drop a Tinderbox file onto your favorite text editor, and you'll see text you can read and tags that make sense. That in itself is a great comfort: if worse comes to worst, if Tinderbox suddenly vanished completely as if it had never been, your data would still be yours.

Working Things Out

Notes play three distinct roles in our daily work:

- Notes are *records*, reminding us of ideas and observations that we might otherwise forget.
- Shared notes are a *medium*, an efficient communication channel between colleagues and collaborators.
- Notes are a *process* for clarifying thinking and for refining inchoate ideas.

Significance often emerges gradually from the accumulation of factual detail and from our growing understanding of the relationships among isolated details. Only after examining the data, laying it out and handling it, can we feel comfortable in reaching complex decisions.

For example, suppose we need to examine the marketplace for, say, digital cameras. Perhaps we need a new camera ourselves: which do we purchase? Perhaps we have decided to provide a camera to each member of our company's outside sales team, so that when they encounter a special situation – an awkward installation requirement that needs special attention from Engineering, or a damaged shipment that demands action from Fulfillment in addition to smoothing a customer's ruffled feathers – our representative will always have a camera handy to document the problem. Or, perhaps we're planning to bundle our next product with a camera and need to select the most appropriate strategic partner.

At first, we might scan a magazine survey of current cameras, jotting down some notes about the most popular and interesting models. Additional research – visiting stores, asking colleagues, checking what other companies in your field are buying – might yield additional possibilities.

Sooner or later, of course, you'll have too much data, too many options each clamoring for attention. We need to add some structure to our notes, a preliminary organization. At this stage, however, we know very little about the problem. Our organizational scheme needs to be simple to implement and easy to change, since committing too early to a rigid organization is bound to lead to extra work, and could even prejudice the outcome or lead us to overlook good approaches that don't fit neatly into our flawed initial structure.

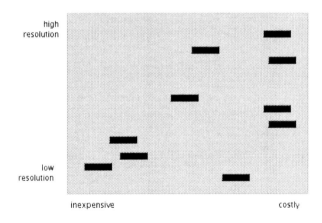

Figure 1. A Tinderbox map organizes cameras by resolution and price.

Here, we have quickly arranged our notes in a simple, informal chart, much as we might lay out a few note cards on the top of our desk. Here, we're plotting the tradeoff between cost and image quality; in general, we expect lower-resolution cameras to be less expensive than their newer, higher-resolution brethren.

The correlation isn't perfect, though. Why are some low-resolution cameras more costly? Some manufacturers spend money on rugged construction to withstand rough handling and extreme temperatures. We'll add a border to highlight the ruggedized cameras.

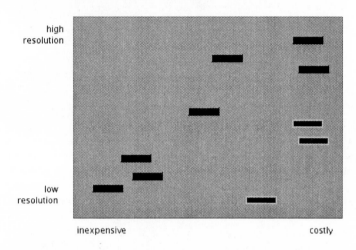

Figure 2. The cameras in the lower-right sector seem at first to be poor value. We find, however, that their manufacturers invest in rugged construction rather than resolution.

Additional digging uncovers more kinds of cameras. These vary in cost and resolution, of course, but they also vary in other ways. Some cameras are exceptionally small; we'll make smaller notes for these. Others are designed for teleconferencing; we'll use a lighter color for these.

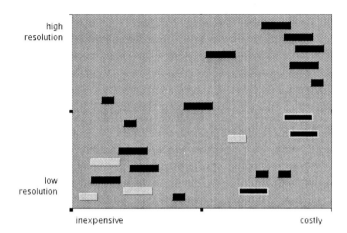

Figure 3. Some cameras (light gray) are intended chiefly for teleconferencing. Others are notably compact and are represented as smaller squares. As the map becomes more elaborate, our understanding of the problem space improves.

Alert to unexpected differentiators, we continue to notice that some cameras don't fit our expected pattern. One costly camera is especially stylish. Some cameras use standard, widely available lenses. Others use smaller, lighter optics specifically designed for digital cameras. Some can accept infrared filters popular in art photography; this seems an irrelevant frill until Field Engineering complains (again) that improper installation of your products is leading to premature failure due to overheating. Perhaps the sales crew can check this in the course of routine visits?

Our Tinderbox notes are accumulating detail and growing in representational depth and completeness. At the same time, our own understanding of the problem space – of the camera industry, its problems and tradeoffs and the different approaches of the major players – is increasing.

Often, that understanding proves much more valuable than the data itself, *but the understanding cannot be acquired without the data*. If we're planning to equip every member of a large sales force with a camera, the approval and procurement process might well require months. We might not have a good opportunity to distribute the cameras and train the salespeople until the annual sales conference. By the time we actually place the order, most of the cameras in our initial notes will be obsolete, replaced by newer models with different characteristics at different price points. What will not have changed, in all probability, is the picture of the industry and the engineering requirements we formed in our study. The actual camera model we'll eventually purchase has not yet been designed.

What we learn from our notes is not that the Z15 is a better value than the MR42. We learn what the camera designers are trying to do, and we learn what we really need. We learn, in short, how to make the decision.

Notetaking can be like sketching, a private exercise to improve the acuity of our perception and to focus our understanding. Our sketches often focus on small detail: a study of a hand, say, or the weathered wood of porch behind a Gloucester drug store. We don't draw these studies because we expect the image to matter, but because sketching these things with care and attention will improve our eye. By learning to draw the hand or the mountain, we polish our ability to draw anything. The process, not the picture, matters.

Note: Kumiyo Nakakoji (University of Tokyo) calls this *representational talkback*. The writer seeks a way to represent the problem space, sketches notes that describe an initial approach, and then reviews the notes as if approaching the problem anew. If the representation is good, the problem now seems simpler. If the representation fails to make sense, that incoherence often suggests a new and better approach to the problem. Nakakoji's studies of tools for enhancing this internal dialog, *Amplified Representational Talkback,* influenced the design of Tinderbox.

Conceptual Clustering

In choosing a camera, we progressed from readily-accessible but excessively concrete information – today's camera models – to improve our understanding of camera selection and, indeed, of the digital camera industry. We used notes to focus our attention and to discover patterns and exceptions.

Tinderbox maps are equally useful for getting a handle on complex, abstract issues where a wealth of competing abstractions threatens to overwhelm us, and where facts seem scarce.

Consider, for example, the problems inherent in planning a critical meeting that brings together important people for a very limited time. The participants might be the corporate sales force at their annual meeting, or an international panel of researchers gathered to discuss the policy implications of recent discoveries, a policy summit of a political party, or a program committee of an academic conference. In planning any of these events, we're faced with a host of things we might want to address. So many, indeed, that it is easy to become paralyzed by the enormous number of possibilities. Where to begin? When all topics are vitally important, how can we start at the beginning or decide which comes first?

One useful approach to analysis paralysis is to temporarily abandon analysis. Instead, we simple gather a map of concepts, topics, ideas, and proposals. At first, we make no attempt at all to organize these suggestions: the first goal is to capture all the ideas, to ensure that everything we might want to consider is represented in the map.

Figure 4. Weblog researcher Jack Vinson studies an ad hoc concept map for the Blogwalk 2005 conference. Each slip represents a proposed discussion topic; different colors represent distinct contributors. Tinderbox maps are more flexible than blizzard-cooled windows, and preserve a permanent record for later use.

Inevitably, we'll find that the map contains some duplicate suggestions. Since the map layout at present is arbitrary, we'll simply move one of the duplicates close to the other.

Sometimes, two suggestions will be distinct and yet their relationship will immediately be clear. In some cases, the difference may be terminological; the two topics are similar but the words describing them differ. In some cases, one suggestion subsumes the other. Again, we can gather related items together, perhaps clearing space by moving unrelated items someplace else.

At times, one note might seem to belong to two distinct clusters. Often, this suggests that the two clusters are related. Perhaps they are better represented as a single cluster. Alternatively, we might position the problematic notes *between* two distinct clusters.

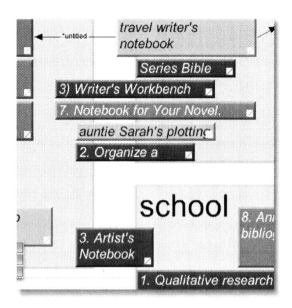

Figure 5. An excerpt from one of the first Tinderbox maps ever created, a planning document for Tinderbox applications. The "Artist's Notebook" bridges distinct but related application clusters.

Tinderbox maps give you lots of latitude for expressing relationships among clusters. You can merge two clusters that seem indistinguishable. If the clusters are distinct but related, you might move them together. In time, groups of clusters (metaclusters) often emerge to represent broad themes. At other times, the linkage is important but extrinsic; the two clusters are not, in fact, closely related beyond this common element. Links are often ideal for representing these connections. Finally, the same item might appear separately in two or more different contexts. This is an ideal opportunity to use Tinderbox aliases.

On occasion, conceptual clustering breaks down. The clusters we formed seem increasingly arbitrary, or excessively rigid, or we're left with one amorphous cluster and numerous isolated outliers. The best approach in such situations is sometimes to shuffle the cards and start over.

First, save a copy of the map. The current clustering might eventually seem less unsatisfactory than it does now.

Next, use one of the Tinderbox map's Cleanup commands to uncluster the diagram you've built. If that's not sufficient, consider sorting the items in some artificial order – alphabetically, perhaps, or by creation time.

Now, take a break. Get away from the screen, take a walk, and work on something else for a few minutes. Relax. On returning, consider adding a few new items that might have been overlooked before. Then, and only then, try to find a new relationship or two at the outset; try to avoid recreating the initial process. Once you have found a handful of new relationships, you won't need to worry about the old organization reasserting itself.

Notes about Notes

WRITE IT DOWN

Take notes to learn. Many people find that notetaking gives you an opportunity to reflect, to fix new ideas in your mind. Making notes helps you focus and concentrate. The care and attention that notetaking demands – whether you're finding the right language to describe an idea or seeking the right line to capture an image – helps you see more clearly and understand more completely.

Take notes to remember. Time flies: someday, you'll want to remember this. Your notes become a record of ideas and moods, of goals and accomplishments. You want to write down the appointment you just made for next Tuesday, because you'll need to remember it Tuesday – and because your grandchildren might just be glad to know about it, too.

Take notes to explore. It's a big world, a world that's more open to your exploration than ever before. As you travel about town or across the globe, you'll want to record your impressions – both to get the most out of every day, and to look back on later. You'll be back in Paris again, but you'll never again see Paris for the very first time.

And that client you met today? That might be the start of a crucial partnership that might last years or decades.

Take notes to create. Doodle. Sketch. Try out different styles, and new voices.

Above all, remember to write it down.

IMPROVE THE MOMENT

There is never enough time, in part because we are always waiting. Waiting for appointments, waiting for others to arrive or to join us, waiting for airplanes and trains and phone calls.

If you always have a pen, you can use spare moments to write.

Although I don't draw well, I enjoy drawing people I see in cafés and airports. Nothing you do is going to make flight 174 leave sooner, and you'll have plenty of time to read (and perhaps to work on your weekly sweep) while you're sitting on the plane. Airports are a fine place for observation and exploration; in airports, you see people you don't see every day.

> The big international crossroads – Heathrow in London, Changi in Singapore – give you a chance to see people from the far corners of the world, sitting and waiting (like you) for their flights. But small, regional airports offer equally good sketching: you see a lot more cowboys and mining engineers in College Station, Texas, than you're likely to see back home in Boston.

If enforced waiting makes you anxious – especially if you don't know how long the wait may be – you may find waiting to be an opportunity to prep your pages. Short, unpredictable delays can be made less frustrating if you can easily find tasks to improve and organize your work – filling out expense reports, recording details about potential clients, clarifying hastily written passages in your notes. Reserve a page in the front or back of your book, briefly listing pages that are incomplete or unsatisfactory: when you find you must wait for a tardy physician or a slow commuter train, this page can give you plenty of worthwhile things to improve the moment.

YOU NEED TWO JOURNALS

You need **two** places to write. One should be ready-to-hand all the time. When you wake up in the middle of the night with a great idea, you need someplace to write it down so you won't have forgotten it by the morning. When you're in traffic and suddenly see an unexpected connection, you need to be able to pull over, park, and capture the idea. When someone tells you about a great book or a terrific new restaurant, don't try to remember: write it down.

> If you make lots of appointments, you also need a calendar. Your calendar or PDA is for scheduling time: don't try to use your calendar ToDo list as a place for all your notes.

These spur-of-the-moment notes can be written in a nice, small notebook. Others prefer to use note cards, or the back of business cards, or a clipboard. In reaction to elaborate PDAs, some computer pros now call a deck of 3x5 cards a "Hipster PDA".

You also need a **permanent repository** for your notes – a place where all your notes can be safely stored, reviewed, and acted on. Every day or every week, you'll want to move your quick jottings from your Hipster PDA or your pocket notebook into your repository. A good journal makes a fine repository. A powerful content assistant like Tinderbox works well, too.

ALWAYS HAVE A PEN

Always have a pen, and always have something to write on. You can't take notes if your tools aren't ready to hand. Trying to remember what you will want to write down later *increases* your anxiety and workload, defeating the purpose of your notebook.

You need **both** low tech and high tech journal tools. You need to have a reliable paper notebook that's always handy and available instantly – and you need a pen or pencil that's equally available. This notebook need not be large – for some people, a handful of blank cards is sufficient – but it needs to be within reach in the middle of the night, in your car, in the elevator. Its purpose is simple: to capture ideas and other things you need to remember. Write them down at once: don't try to remember.

These paper notes need to be swept regularly into a permanent storage system – a tool like Tinderbox that lets you preserve, organize, and analyze all your notes.

The more accessible your major notebook, the easier you'll find it to sweep your notes into it and to reorganize and study those notes. That means you'll want to bring your computer along to meetings and you'll want to pack it on trips.

You need **at least** two cases for every laptop computer. One, a conventional laptop bag, briefcase or backpack, needs to hold spare batteries, cables, accessories, and chargers – everything you'll need for an extended trip. A second, minimalist case should give you a lightweight way to carry your computer when you're just going down the hall or heading across campus.

GOOD HOME

Your notes are important. Even if your notes are simply scratch work for software development or memos about when to pick up the soccer team, they represent a real investment of care and attention.

Time is short. You spend time making notes; those moments should be as pleasurable as you can make them. And the more durable, enjoyable, and attractive your notes may be, the better the chance that you'll continue to find them useful – and that your biographer or your grandchildren will enjoy them as well.

The cost of even the finest, most luxurious and durable journal is negligible when compared to your investment in writing it – and the loss you'll face if you lose or discard your journal.

If investing in good paper and a good cover help you enjoy your
notes, you'll be more likely to keep them.

WEEKLY SWEEP

You need two journals: one that can be always handy (and which is
often on paper) and one that is permanent, intelligent, and easy to
search. Tinderbox is ideal for your permanent information store.

Sweep all your paper notes into your Tinderbox file periodically –
every morning, or once a week.

It's important to establish the habit of writing things down
immediately, and just as important to establish a rhythm of moving
these jottings into your permanent store. The purpose of the weekly
sweep is not improving or editing or polishing, though some people
like to do a little cleaning as they copy. The point is twofold:

- One purpose of writing things down is to remember, to
  make the information and ideas available to you later. The
  weekly sweep lets you reflect on your recent ideas and
  decide which ideas need to be pursued immediately.
- By moving things into a smart and permanent storage
  medium, you make them available for searching and for
  analysis. Your Tinderbox can automatically scan, categorize,
  and sort ideas, and Tinderbox maps and attributes can help
  you discover patterns and reveal structure. Fast search and
  secure backup ensure that you'll be able to find your notes
  later and that you'll have them handy when you need them.

Get into the habit. Scan the drawings, transcribe the text. Get your
material where you can search it, scan it, organize it.

3. Lists and Containers

Task Lists

Tinderbox map views help you gather, cultivate, and analyze new information. At times, though, nothing beats a list. Lists are particularly helpful when the challenge is not to capture information but rather to decide which information is most important.

For example, consider the simple task list. In a busy world, everyone has too much to do and too much to remember. At times, we may have so many tasks to finish and errands to run that it's hard to know where to start.

The Tinderbox outline view is a superb list manager. You can make a new note quickly: just press **Return** and type its title. Press **Return** again, and you've got another note.

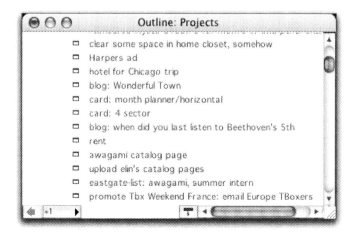

Figure 6. A small part of a task list.

I keep a Tinderbox file of *projects* I've undertaken, or that I'd like to undertake someday. Right now, I've got 34 active projects and another 38 projects on which I'd like to get started if I can find time or resources. Active projects range from personal tasks like paying bills to Tinderbox design and development, from our ongoing kitchen renovations to supervising computer science research. Writing this book is one of those 34 projects.

I know that I have 34 active projects, because I've made a list – and because Tinderbox makes it easy to count them.

Hint: to count the number of notes in a container, select the container and choose **Get Info** from the Note menu (cmd-I)

Note: this is an unusually small number of active projects. I've just consolidated some groups of projects into single large projects, because I suspected they could be divided up in a more useful way, and I've got about fifty projects queued up for admission to the queue. But 35 projects gives me a chance to spend a chunk of time looking at each project every week or so; if I had 160 active projects, some would be untouched for weeks on end.

There are only about 110 waking hours in the work week.

In the same file, I have a container called **Current** that contains specific tasks I'd like to do as soon as I can manage them. Another container, called **Done**, collects tasks that I have completed; when I finish a task, I drag it from Current to Done. I've got 165 current tasks. I finished 879 tasks in the past 50 weeks, which suggests that the contents of Current turns over every two months.

Extreme Programming adherents use statistics like these to create a rough measure of *work velocity*. Not all the tasks in Current are equivalently important or equally ambitious, and each requires different amounts of time and resources. But if I find that, in a typical month I finish about 75 tasks, then a month in which I finish

120 tasks (or only finish 45 tasks) might suggest that I've changed my working habits – or that the kind of work I'm doing has changed.

> **Caution**: Remember that averages are simply averages; if in a typical month I finish 75 tasks, statistical fluctuation alone is likely to let me finish about 84 tasks in some months and only 66 tasks in other. If your velocity is **n** tasks a month, you should probably anticipate fluctuations of roughly sqrt(n) tasks as a matter of chance and happenstance.

> Remember, too, that velocity changes might well arise from an influx of small, easy tasks, or from a subtle change in the way you decide where one task ends and another begins. It's easy to game the system. Velocity is a useful hint, but a poor criterion for evaluating your staff.

> Be careful not to invest energy in gaming the system simply to fool yourself. Measurement is good, because knowing more is good, but if you become emotionally or financially invested in the measurement – if your annual bonus depends on your task velocity – the value of measure will be quickly eclipsed by the incidental damage it causes.

The Problem with PDAs

Handheld or palm-top computers offer superb tools for managing calendars and contacts. These tools almost always include a ToDo list, to which you can easily add tasks you intend to accomplish. Having completed a task, you can handily check it off as finished. Unfinished tasks are automatically rolled over from day to day until they're finished.

PDA ToDo lists should only be used for tasks you need to accomplish on a specific day. For example, if you are scheduled to make a presentation to the board of directors on February 3, you might well want to remind yourself to review your presentation on February 2. It doesn't matter whether you do this in the morning or afternoon, as long as you remember to do it. You might know about the presentation months in advance, long before you have much idea what your schedule for the previous day will look like; you don't need to *schedule* a specific appointment. You do know, however, that you want to set aside an hour at some point of the day. This is the ideal role for the PDA ToDo list.

It's tempting to use PDA lists for everything we want to do. This is almost always a mistake.

First, you have too much to do. If you're honest with yourself, and thorough, at any given moment you have hundreds and hundreds of things that you want and intend to do. Some are simple tasks – pick up groceries after work, request a raise, decide whether to hold next year's user conference in Boston or San Francisco. Others are compound projects made up of many smaller tasks (finish that novel you've been meaning to write), or require research (find out what my niece would like for her birthday), or demand contemplation (should I change careers?). Some tasks must be done soon (change the oil), others might require an indefinite wait for someone else to finish their assignment (once Judy agrees to get married, plan the wedding).

Most people can easily identify several hundred tasks they need, want, or expect to do[1]. The screen of your PDA can display only a dozen or so tasks at a time. The whole point of the PDA is its portability, and that very portability only works for you if you keep your portable lists small.

Just as important, **the wrong things end up on the list**. Most crucially, sooner or later you'll add to your ToDo list some things that you *should* do, but that you don't especially want to do, and that are not especially urgent. Tasks like this, once on a ToDo list, tend to stay there forever, getting older and older. Every time you look at your ToDo list, it reminds you: that's what the ToDo list is for. But now, instead of reminding you of your immediate and urgent needs, it's filled with unimportant and distasteful chores. Soon, the ToDo list becomes a guilt attractor, too horrible to contemplate.

Of course, this completely obviates the utility of the ToDo list. If every glance at the list inspires frustration, impatience, and guilt, then naturally we'll avoid looking at it. And, if we don't look at it, the ToDo list can no longer be trusted to remind us of those things we absolutely need to accomplish on a specific day. Sooner or later, in the rush of urgent work and tired of the list's incessant nagging about filling out paperwork or scheduling dental checkups, we'll forget to rehearse a major presentation or fail to send a tax deposit.

The answer is simple: reserve the ToDo list in your PDA or desk planner for tasks that need to be accomplished on a specific day. That means almost every task in your PDA will be finished on the day it's scheduled, and tasks will roll over only in unusual circumstances – sick days, unexpected emergencies, crises – and will always be resolved soon afterward.

Where do you put the hundreds of other tasks in your ToDo list? In Tinderbox, of course.

Plan Priorities, Not Schedules

In managing a list of all the many hundreds of things we need, want or intend to do, our problem is not chiefly the matter of scheduling. We already know there's too much to do, that there's never going to be enough time for everything. We don't need a PDA or a PERT chart to tell us this. What we need is *analysis*. We need to know what we want to do soon, what needs to be done eventually, and we need to know what to do first.

Tinderbox is well adapted to this sort of analysis. A comprehensive examination of all the tasks we want to address is likely to run to hundreds or thousands of items, and reviewing a task may well remind us of even more tasks that lead up to it or that should follow in its wake. It's easy to make, add, and organize notes in Tinderbox. Because Tinderbox notes are lightweight objects, we can work with thousands. Tinderbox's many views give you many different perspectives on your tasks; you can zoom into a small section of urgent items in an outline, cluster dozens of related tasks in a map, or use a treemap to step back and get a mountain-top perspective on everything. Fast search and agents help you find forgotten or misplaced tasks, and links can help keep related tasks connected.

Using PDAs to plan leads you to focus on time. Your itinerary is important – it's inconvenient to miss the boat – but you don't want to make all your connections only to find that your journey has taken you one place when you would more profitably have traveled somewhere else.

Tip: The small screen size of PDAs exerts a constant torque, silently urging you to keep task descriptions short and to avoid having many tasks. This, too, defeats the utility of ToDo lists.

Consider, for example, the planning required for a business trip. If I've agreed to speak at a conference in London, there are some things I simply have to do. I *must* get plane tickets, I *must* arrange for a hotel, and I *must* send the title and abstract of the talk to the conference organizers. If these things don't get done, the trip won't happen at all.

But the presence of that trip on the schedule suggests a variety of planning tasks that *might* lead to good things. Do I have customers or prospects in London whom I should visit? Old colleagues or classmates I'd enjoy seeing again? Are there restaurants I should try, or museums I should visit, or Londoners I've always wanted to meet? None of these are absolutely essential – I might not have time, before the trip, to explore each of these tasks. But, if I do have a moment or two to spare, why not invest it in planning?

Look broadly at the people and places involved – your colleagues, the people you will be visiting, the events you will be attending, and other things and people you can see while there or *en route*.

Finding Priorities

I have 165 tasks in my Current list. That's too many to remember, too many to see on the screen, and too many to print legibly on a page. Moreover, the first purpose of the task list is simply to tell me what I should do next. How do I choose which task is the most important task to undertake right now?

First, some tasks can only be done at certain places. I can only make progress on my closet problems if I'm at home. My mother lives in Chicago; I can't repair her easel if I'm in Boston. When a constraint like this crops up often, I use an agent or a rule to color-code the task.

Second, some things (weekly meetings, doctor appointments) need to be done at specific times. These go straight into my calendar. Mixing tasks and appointments increases guilt and confusion; separating them helps focus your attention and anxiety where it will do the most good.

Some tasks don't need to be scheduled, but are still associated with a deadline or timeframe. If a task has a deadline, I'll write the effective due date in a Tinderbox attribute named Reminder. An agent scans for notes in Current that have a Reminder set within the next week; these are tasks I need to watch.

Finally, we're left with perhaps 100 additional tasks. Finding *the* most important single task in a long list is daunting, but bringing some order to the list is not difficult.

1. Examine the first two items on the list. If one is clearly more important than the other, move it up on the list.
2. Examine the next pair of items. Swap them if the second is more important than the first. If either item is exceptionally important, give it a boost near the top of the list. If either item is exceptionally unimportant, move it down the list – or send it back to its project, removing it from the Current tasks entirely.
3. Continue to the end of the list. Repeat a few times.

After two or three passes, the important tasks will be concentrated near the top of the list, and the less important tasks will be concentrated near the bottom.

To finish polishing the list, scan down the list until you find a note that is clearly positioned too low. Select it. Press cmd-up-arrow (Move Up in the Note menu) to move it higher in the list. Continue pressing cmd-up-arrow until (a) you bump into a note that's even more important, or (b) you reach the top of the list. Now, find a note that is clearly too high in the list. Press cmd-down-arrow repeatedly until the note you're moving bumps into a note with even lower priority.

Once you're confident that all the most crucial tasks are near the top, you can focus on sorting the top dozen tasks. Or, just take one of those tasks, do it, and move on.

Bags, Bunches, and Sequences

Tinderbox containers can play three distinct roles in organizing your information. Lists are a simple concept, so simple indeed that Tinderbox users seldom ask many questions about them. Nonetheless, it can be useful to think carefully about their different roles.

First, a container may simply represent a collection of things, gathered together in one place.

- People to whom you want to send holiday cards
- Your instant messaging "buddy list"
- The list of Web pages you'd like to read, when you find the time
- The groceries you want to purchase after work
- The membership list of the company's graphic standards committee

These collections are *bags* or "piles", a set of notes without any particular order and which are individually significant. The importance of a bag is simply that it collects some notes that will be useful in a particular context. When your work brings that context into focus, you can open the bag and see all the relevant notes. When the context is irrelevant, you simply file that bag away.

Second, we have *bunches* – lists of notes that are interesting or useful to us primarily as composite collections rather than individual notes. For example, suppose you manage a team that, from time to time, announces your company's new products to the industry press. When a new product is ready to roll out, you need to determine which staff members are responsible for briefing various reporters, writers, and analysts. In all, hundreds of people need to be contacted and briefed; to facilitate this, you might break down "the press" into a collection of bunches:

- Analysts, Wall Street
- Analysts, International
- Newspapers, Eastern US region
- Newspapers, Western US region
- Trade Journals
- Strategic partner executives: US
- Strategic partner executives: Asia

Instead of assigning personnel to handle a list of individuals, this lets you easily treat a bundle of people and publications as a unit. "Alice will handle the Wall Street analysts, and Bob will handle all the other analysts and the Asian partners."

Finally, we often encounter lists where the individual items in the list are important, and where the order in which they appear is significant. These ordered lists are *sequences*. Some common examples might include

- Weblog posts, in reverse chronological order
- Purchase requisitions, by date of request
- Procedures and checklists

Tinderbox provides useful facilities for bags, bunches, and sequences. Bags are often best viewed in a Tinderbox map window; to open an extra map window, select the container and choose **New Map View** from the Views menu. When you're finished, you can put the bag away by closing the window. If you prefer a more compact display, you can select the bag and choose **New Outline View** from the Views menu to open a new window that lists only the contents of the bag.

By collapsing a *bunch* in outline view, you can easily move or manipulate all the items in a container with a single gesture. Actions and Rules can be useful for enforcing constraints among all the notes in a bunch. For example, if your bundle of "Wall Street Analysts" has the OnAdd action

Color=$Color(parent)

then any note added to this bundle will have the same color as the
container.

Adornments and Containers

Tinderbox maps provide two ways of grouping notes in collections:
adornments and containers.

Adornments appear in the background layer of maps, and are hidden
in other views. They help organize and annotate the space of the
map, emphasizing and clarifying some spatial relationships.

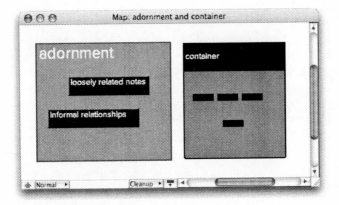

Figure 7. Adornments express loose and experimental relationships, while
containers express more concrete and lasting ideas of subordination or
containment.

It is easy to move items onto adornments, and just as easy to move
them partly or completely away. Part of a note might lie on one
adornment, and part on another. Tinderbox users sometimes speak of
adornments as signposts, describing a note as "not far from the big
red adornment". Adornments are best at expressing tentative and
contingent relationships.

Placing notes inside a container is more emphatic, indicating some
confidence in assigning the note. Containers have cleaner semantics: a
note is either inside a container, or it is not. Containers hide some of
the details of their contents; they can be collapsed in charts and

outlines, and links into containers are abbreviated in map view. By hiding their details, containers let you focus attention on their role as a bunch.

Sorting Lists Automatically

Containers also provide important tools for managing lists. Most significantly, containers can sort their contents.

Don't overlook opportunities to use container sorting to help organize your work. Note that the sort order is significant for the map's Clean Up... commands; often, you may sort a container as a prelude to using the Clean Up... menu.

Sorting is fast, and changing sorting criteria is easy. Often, you may want to take a quick peek at a new sort criterion – for example, to see the delegated project that is most seriously overdue. Simply change the sort criteria temporarily, and then change them back. (If the new criteria turn out to be especially useful, consider creating an agent that looks for notes #inside(the container) and that sorts those notes using the new criteria.)

Container and Adornment Actions

Containers can also perform actions on notes when they are added to the container. These actions are often quite simple – for example, the container CompletedTasks might mark each task as Finished when the task is dragged into the container. Several simple actions may be chained together, separated by semicolons:

Date=today; Status=Complete; Color=;

Adornments perform actions, just as containers do. Containers act on a note when the note is created in or added to the container, while adornments perform actions when a note is moved onto the adornment.

Note: adornment actions are applied to all notes
that touch some part of the adornment, and are
reapplied when a note is dragged to a new location
touching the adornment.

Container and adornment actions help automate routine tasks. For
example, what happens to tasks on your ToDo list once you have
completed them? You could simply delete those tasks, of course, but
retaining them could have useful benefits:

- We retain a record that the task has been finished,
  rather than forgotten or mislaid.
- The time when we marked the task as completed can be
  useful if, at some later time, we need to investigate or
  review the task or find information about it for
  colleagues, vendors, or managers.
- Reviewing and analyzing old ToDo items may provide
  useful information for project post-mortems or future
  planning and budgeting decisions.

The cost of retaining old ToDo items is modest: they require a little
extra storage space, they need to be examined by agents (and so make
agents a little bit slower), and inconsistent or "dirty" items can create
confusion. If we find a ToDo task that is marked as Completed but is
still filed with Current Tasks, does that mean the task still needs to be
done (and that its marking as Completed is spurious) or that the task
was indeed completed (and is now misfiled)?

We can help reduce or eliminate inconsistent metadata by using
container actions to enforce constraints and to assert metadata.
Working by hand, the workflow for marking a task as completed
might be tedious:

1. Set **Completed** to true
2. Set **CompletionTime** to the current
   date and time
3. Remove any special color coding we
   applied to this task
4. File under FinishedTasks

Each element of this workflow increases the likelihood that something will be forgotten, leaving the document in an inconsistent state.

Instead, Tinderbox lets us reduce the complexity to a single step:

1.   File under FinishedTasks

The container of FinishedTasks automatically performs the other steps when it receives a new task:

OnAdd: Completed=true;CompletionTime="today";Color=;

These steps are applied when a note is added, and so they can be overridden later when exceptions arise. For example, on Tuesday a customer reported a missing order.

Current Tasks

Trace Johnson order TX-183

We look into the matter, find the parcel is scheduled for delivery later that afternoon, and pass the information to the customer. The task is completed, and we place it in CompletedTasks.

Several days later, the customer inquires again: where is our package? You investigate and discover that the delivery truck went to the wrong location, and that the parcel is waiting at the factory receiving room when it ought to have been delivered to Johnson's downtown offices. You call the customer to explain, confirm that the problem is now resolved, and update the task's CompletionTime by hand.

Automate To Reduce Tedium

Add actions to containers and adornments whenever you notice that
moving a note to a new place also suggests or requires other actions,
such as updating time stamps or changing colors.

Repetitive workflow is tedious and prone to error. You have
important things to do; let your Tinderbox document assist you by
taking on repetitive work. Experience shows repeatedly that, when
people are expected or required to add metadata to documents, they
will find interesting ways to avoid performing this dull, unrewarding
chore. Once you discover that some of your metadata are incomplete
or incorrect, it becomes difficult to rely on any of the metadata – and
still more difficult to expend extra time and energy on adding and
maintaining the metadata.

Conversely, don't spend much time automating exceptional cases.
Exceptions are rare; it's harder to regain the time you spend on
automation if the case is unusual. Also, exceptions are interesting;
you're more likely to notice exceptions and won't mind occasional
manual work.

Lists: Past and Future

Making and managing lists is clearly part of our personal information
management regimen. Lists are common; we need good ways to
represent them and to work with them. Too often, we treat lists as
long lists of text and try to manage them with word processors.
Sometimes, we treat lists as truncated tables and try to manage them
with spreadsheets. But lists aren't a special, degenerate case of texts
and tables; lists deserve tools that understand lists.

Notice, in particular, how Tinderbox lists keep track
of the way they sort themselves. Sorting isn't
applied to a Tinderbox list when it is finished, since
you can never know when your notes *are* finished.
When you revise or extend a list in Tinderbox, the
list can automatically sort itself.

Similarly, actions and rules let you extend the
semantics of a list.

Make lots of lists. Books you've read. Books you *want* to read. Make lists of films you've seen, restaurants you've enjoyed, wines you've tasted.

At minimum, you may someday treasure these lists as mementos. You'll be able to look back, a year from now, and think about the movies of the year: Did you see too many clunkers? Do you wish you'd seen more movies that won awards? Or would you rather see fewer Hollywood blockbusters next year, and spend the time revisiting classics instead? And won't it be interesting to revisit this list in five years? In twenty-five?

These lists are letters to your future self, but the same lists can make wonderful weblog features. They provide an unobtrusive and graceful way to share your intellectual and artistic interests with your friends and relatives.

You might ask: "Why would anyone be interested in what I'm reading? Isn't that terribly egotistical?" But, surely, your mother would be interested. Your nieces and nephews, sisters, cousins, and aunts might like to know. Your college roommate might wonder, now and then, what you're doing these days – not the career notes they publish in the alumni bulletin, but what you're really enjoying and what you're thinking about. I have a cousin I get to visit every year or so, and whenever I walk into her house she's got a half-dozen books scattered on her coffee table and one of those books is always something I immediately want to read. I'd love to know what she's reading the rest of the year.

Of course, if we all telephoned our nephews and our cousins whenever we read a book or saw a movie, we'd spend all our time on the phone. By posting lists on the Web, we make them available for sharing by those who are interested, when they are interested.

4. Attributes and Values

Regular Information

A *regular polygon* is a symmetrical shape with sides of equal length, such as a square or a hexagon. By analogy, we say that *regular information* occurs in fixed and predictable patterns, where each item contains the same components.

We are accustomed to using databases to deal with *regular* information. A register of personal checks, for example, has a regular structure: each check necessarily contains specific kinds of information:

Bank name

Account number

Check number

Payee

Amount

Signature

[memorandum]

Every check we write is drawn on exactly one bank, for precisely one amount, and each has exactly one check number. If we need to record checks, we don't need to worry about checks that are not drawn on a bank, or where "check number" is not a number, or where "Amount" is a poem or a drawing.

Regular information possesses qualities that help us store and process it with great efficiency. Because each item is regular, its size and its components can be predicted in advance; if we want to "reserve space for storing 1000 checks", we can do this without much thought. Because every check has the same structure, we can often find ways to store checks very efficiently and to access information about checks very quickly.

Databases are computer systems for storing and retrieving large amounts of regular information. The strength of the database is speed and efficiency, but its drawback is inflexibility. Because regular data can be analyzed and understood, databases reward advance analysis and systematic planning. When we create a database application to manage personal checks, we begin by listing the fields that describe a check, and because checks are well understood we can reasonably expect that we can successfully anticipate what fields we will require. Databases work best when our initial analysis is complete and correct; if our understanding of the data changes radically in the course of development, we usually need to start over.

Because checks are regular, it's also easy for the computer to sort them in various ways and to search very efficiently. By keeping checks sorted, we can answer some queries ("Find check #7231") without having to examine every check. Because we understand check semantics, we can track our total expenditures to identify exceptionally large or small transactions that might deserve special attention, and we can easily compute our bank balance or report total expenditures for last month.

Much of the information we encounter, in business and elsewhere, is regular, but much of it is not. Some irregularities begin as exceptions, situations that standard forms nearly accommodate but don't quite capture. We may need to keep track of things that are nearly checks, but not quite – post-dated checks that represent casual loans, payment vouchers, IOUs, accounts receivable, markers, and certificates promising breakfast in bed to the Birthday Girl. We may need to catalog things we never anticipated, as when an accountant discovered that her client – a famous artist, recently deceased – was in the habit of sketching witty portraits on the face of cancelled checks and had bequeathed this collection to a university art museum. We may need to augment the anticipated information with an entirely new galaxy of data if, for example, we need to pore through a murder victim's checkbook for information that might suggest a motive.

All these cases start with the same, regular data, but each develops unique needs and extensions. Databases place great weight on getting the structure exactly right from the beginning, so that they can be as fast and efficient as possible. Here, we cannot hope to know what we need in advance. And, if speed and efficiency require extensive re-engineering whenever we discover new requirements, then speed and efficiency can't be our chief concern. Often, we'd greatly prefer to make it easier to adapt our system quickly – even if our software will run a little less swiftly.

Irregular Information

The notes and data we accumulate in our inbox, or in the course of doing research, are irregular and unstructured. They store information that is meaningful to us, but nearly opaque to the computer.

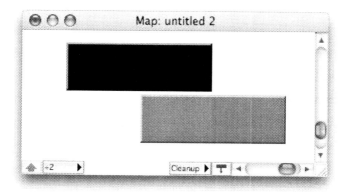

Figure 8. Notes without any metadata are nearly opaque to the computer. They may, however, mean something to us: our habits in coloring and arranging notes may tell us a lot about these objects.

Consider a collection of notes I make in the course of a workday. Perhaps some notes represent ideas I have jotted in meetings. Of these, some might relate to the subject matter of the meeting, reflecting ideas discussed or resolutions adopted by the participants, while other notes might describe ideas that came to me while I happened to be in the meeting. Some notes might be email and phone messages awaiting my attention. Still others are snapshots I captured this morning with my digital camera, poems my niece wrote last week, and reminders for my next expense report.

Because this data is irregular, the computer has to work harder to store it and, once stored, the computer can do much less with it. We can't predict how much space an item will require, and a small note may later become very large:

Reminder: have Bruce paste video from annual meeting here

Usually, there's not much benefit to sorting irregular information. Sorting implies that we compare two things and decide which comes first. But how do we compare a picture of the conference center to last night's dinner receipt, or to the seventh voicemail message waiting for my attention? Because the information is opaque, we can't do much automatic processing or error checking.

Indeed, it might seem that there's not much point in using a computer to work with irregular data at all. But, despite the obstacles, even highly irregular information does offer us some benefits when stored in an environment like Tinderbox:

- Once saved in a computer document, we can make archival copies of the data as often as we like, protecting it from loss or damage.
- Notes can be shared by email, or copied to a CD or DVD that will be delivered to colleagues and collaborators.
- Since Tinderbox files are stored as XML, we can be confident that we'll be able to read them in the future. XML is among the strongest and most widely-deployed standards in computing; if we can read a DVD or locate the file on the Internet in 10, or 50, or 150 years, we should have little trouble extracting our data.
- If some of the information is text, we can search the text for patterns and keywords. This search will not be especially

efficient, since we may need to examine every part of the document, but clever programming (and fast computers) can make it fast enough to be useful.

- We can provide links (Chapter 7) between related items.
- We can put related notes in containers (Chapter 2) to bring related notes together and to facilitate review and retrieval.
- We can build spatial hypertext maps to group related items and to help us locate notes later (Chapter 5).

Though the predictable structure and semantics of regular information make it easier for computers to get leverage, even opaque and irregular information provides plenty of scope for personal assistants.

Everything Is An Attribute

When you write a note in Tinderbox, the program builds data structures to store your information and to facilitate its future use. Some parts of these structures are essentially infrastructure, the plumbing and foundations the software requires for its own use. Others are *metadata* – information the program records because it might perhaps be useful later. Some of the metadata Tinderbox automatically records includes:

- The time and date a note was originally created
- The time and date of the most recent change to the note
- The position of the note in the document outline
- The number of child notes inside the note
- The length of the text in the note, in characters and in words

Tinderbox also needs to store a long list of properties associated with the note, aspects of the note that may affect its appearance or behavior. These might include its color, its map position, the background color to be used for the text and for maps of the note's interior, and many other things.

Tinderbox stores the note's properties and metadata in a long list of attribute-value pairs.

```
Color:    red
Name:     Planck's constant
Created:  1 April 2004
URL:      http://www....]
```

Almost every aspect of a Tinderbox note is ultimately stored as an attribute-value pair.

This simple (and highly regular) structure means that Tinderbox can use a single mechanism for examining any aspect of a note. Whenever Tinderbox needs information about an object in a Tinderbox document, it looks at the object's attribute list and follows a set of rules for finding the value. And, whatever happens, Tinderbox will always find *some* value for any attribute about which it inquires.

Because everything is an attribute, reading and writing Tinderbox notes are largely a matter of reading and writing a list of attributes. This makes Tinderbox's XML files clean and straightforward, and also makes Tinderbox files exceptionally resilient in the face of rapid software development. Because everything is an attribute, it's easy for Tinderbox to grow; the Tinderbox developers can add new behavior and new attributes to support it, and old files continue to work just as they always have.

Attributes aren't simply names; each attribute is an object that knows how to read and to write its values. Different kinds of attributes have different rules for finding and recording their values. Some attributes, such as WordCount, are read-only; you can't set them directly. Others have special inheritance rules – for example, while the values of most attributes can be inherited from a *prototype*, some values (like the name of a note and its map position) are never inherited. Whenever Tinderbox needs to find a value, it follows a simple procedure:

1.   Locate the Attribute object for the desired attribute.
2.   The Attribute object provides methods for finding the corresponding value for the note

The price of the powerful and flexible approach is speed; Tinderbox needs to do extra work whenever it needs to find information about a note. Modern processors, however, are fast enough to handle this without unduly impeding your work.

> **Note**: Tinderbox does a lot of work behind the scenes. For example, simply exporting a weblog may easily involve several million distinct attributes and values, and finding those values may require additional computation to locate inherited values, computed values, and defaults. It turns out that this is precisely the sort of work at which modern processors excel.
>
> Tinderbox is fast enough on today's computers, but would have been impractical on personal computers only a few years ago.

You can add new attributes to a Tinderbox document whenever you like; your attributes are just as powerful (and just as fast) as Tinderbox's built-in attributes. When you define a new attribute, that attribute is immediately a property of every note in the document – new notes and existing notes alike.

> **Note**: Although attributes are always defined for every note in the document, they don't require additional memory for notes that don't use them. Adding a new field to a database often makes the entire database larger and slower, but the impact of adding an attribute is negligible.
>
> Don't hesitate to make new attributes if you need them.

Semi-Structured Information

Often, though we may not be able to anticipate the entire structure that defines an information space, we can easily identify some relevant properties. For example, suppose we are on an airplane, traveling to a conference or trade show. We'll want to take notes during the conference, although we don't yet know precisely what those notes will be or how we'll use them. What we originally expected to be an interesting technical meeting might turn out to be an opportunity to hire some talented people, or to acquire a new product line; your notes will need to be able to adapt to the changing needs of your work.

Whatever the theme of the coming days turns out to be, you'll undoubtedly attend some of the special events, lectures, and presentations that originally led you to the conference.

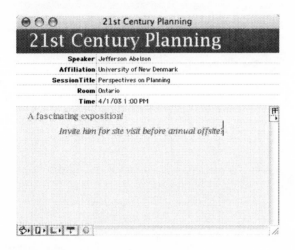

Figure 9. Defining key attributes helps you record information you'll likely want later.

In Figure 9, I've begun my advance preparations with notes to describe events I want to attend. As a first step, I have defined a variety of useful attributes – **Speaker, Affiliation, SessionTitle**, and so forth. You could, of course, include the speaker's name and affiliation in the body of your notes. But by separating out a special area for recording this data, I remind myself to record this information right away.

By adding explicit structure, you also make it easier for Tinderbox to work for you. For example, you might make an agent that searches for notes from any session where Prof. Abelson was a speaker:

AgentQuery: Speaker(Abelson)

This will automatically catalog notes from Abelson's talk; when we attend the second part of his presentation tomorrow, the agent will automatically catalog those notes as well. But the agent won't be confused by other notes that merely mention "Abelson" in the text;

this helps us keep different kinds of notes separate. We don't want
the expense report from lunch with Professor Abelson to be mixed in
with discussions of his research; attributes help us assign just enough
semantic background to let agents distinguish effectively.

Figure 10. This agent searches for all notes in which the Speaker attribute
contains "Abelson". We can more compactly talk about this agent by
simply specifying its query: AgentQuery: Speaker(Abelson)

Attributes also let us collect some kinds of metadata automatically.
For example, we might keep all the notes from one conference session
inside a container:

Perspectives on Planning

21st Century Planning (Abelson)

The Importance of Flexible Plans (Brekke)

Panel: Tools for Better Plan Management (Cruft,
Dotson, Eggert)

If we organize our notes this way, we can easily set some of the
metadata automatically, as soon as a note is created or added to the
session:

OnAdd: SessionTitle=Perspectives on
Planning;Room=Ontario

This kind of *ad hoc* automation requires hardly more work than
simply entering the information once. . Automation saves keystrokes,
but even more importantly it encourages consistency, making notes
easier to find later.

> Note: Prototypes (chapter 5) offer another way to
> automatically assign consistent values. Prototypes
> are ideal where a single note can serve as an
> exemplar for an entire class of notes; a prototypical
> Student, for example, might set a host of attributes
> that would serve as default values for all individual
> students. Actions (and stamps) are ideal when you
> want to set some initial values without establishing a
> permanent connection.

Key Attributes

In principle, every attribute is defined for every note in a Tinderbox
document, but some attributes are especially pertinent to specific
kinds of notes. For example, if some notes represent telephone
messages, such attributes as PhoneNumber will be especially
important. The entire roster of attributes is very long, but it's often
handy to display a few, selected attributes at the top of a note's text
window. We call these *key attributes*.

We can add key attributes individually to a note, by choosing from
the attributes popup menu in the margin of the note's text window
sidebar. Alternatively, you can add key attributes by dragging them
from the attribute palette and dropping them on the text window.
You can also add a group of key attributes at once, by setting the
value of the attribute named **KeyAttributes**. This attribute is simply a
list of attribute names, separated by semicolons:

KeyAttributes:
Caller;Phone;Created;PleaseReturn;WillCallBack

Key attributes can often be instrumental for gradually adding
structure and metadata. Placed at the top of each note, they make it

easy to paste information scattered within the text or implicit in the note's context. In addition, they help communicate what sort of information a note *ought* to contain, and highlight gaps in your information.

Figure 11. Key attributes appear at the top of a note's text window. Often, groups of similar notes will share the same key attributes.

Related kinds of notes often share the same key attributes. Some attributes are pertinent to phone messages, others to library references, and still others to interview notes; an investigative journalist might well keep all three in the same document, with different key attributes for each kind. Key attributes can thus establish a sense of common *type* or *class* among a group of notes.

> **Tip:** When a group of notes share the same key attributes, consider giving them all a common prototype and inheriting the KeyAttribute from that prototype. The prototype can also provide other cues – such as the text background color and typeface in the phone message of Figure 11 to reflect the specific role of the note.

Default Values

How does Tinderbox find the value of a note's attribute?

First, of course, Tinderbox checks to see whether a specific value has been assigned for that note. A specific value can be set in several different ways:

- set explicitly in the text window
- set explicitly in the Get Info window
- set by applying a stamp or a QuickStamp to the note
- set implicitly by a user interface action. For example, resizing a note in a map view implicitly changes its values of Width and Height.
- set automatically by an agent or container action
- set inherently by Tinderbox. For example, Tinderbox always sets the Created timestamp when a new note is added to a document
- computed from the note's properties. For example, the value of Wordcount depends on the note's text, and its OutlinePosition depends on its place in the document.

If no specific value has been assigned, Tinderbox checks to see if the note has a *prototype*. Prototypes are discussed in Chapter 4.

Finally, if Tinderbox is still unable to find the value, Tinderbox uses the attribute's *default* value. The default value is, simply, the value Tinderbox assumes to apply if no other value has been assigned.

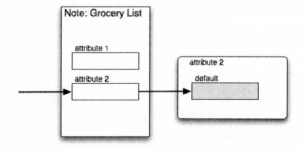

Figure 12. If no value has been assigned to an attribute, Tinderbox instead uses that attribute's *default* value.

USING DEFAULT VALUES

The default values of many System attributes, and of all User attributes, can be changed in the Attributes window.

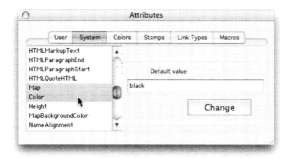

Figure 13. Most default values can be set, or changed, in the Attributes window. For example, the default color for notes can be changed from black to any other color.

Note that changing a default value can affect many notes. If you haven't explicitly set a color for the notes in your document, then changing the default value of Color from black to red will instantly make every note red.

Setting default values can save time and improve your experience. The default size of a newly created note in a map is 1x3, but you can use wider, thinner notes instead by changing the default **Height** and **Width** to 0.5x6. If you want new notes named "titteløs" instead of "untitled", just change the default value of **Name**.

5. Prototypes

Copying and Pasting

Related notes often share many common elements. Telephone messages, for example, often include a name, a time, and a phone number. Bookmarks of Web pages contain a description and a URL. Press releases include a release date, contact information, and a headline.

By understanding these common elements we can save time, and we can use this understanding to improve our notes. Instead of describing each new note from scratch, we can save time and typing by describing the *difference* between the new note and another note that resembles it. Just as important, knowing what information *ought* to be in some kinds of notes can improve efficiency and prevent mistakes; if the phone message form reminds us to get the phone number of the caller every time, we'll have fewer missed connections.

A very simple way to take advantage of common elements among notes is just to duplicate an existing note, and then to edit the copy. Instead of starting with an empty note, we make a duplicate and then describe the differences between the old note and the new one. If the two notes are closely related, the differences will be slight and this simple expedient can save lots of time and typing. The common strategy is familiar from stationery and business forms, and from programs that mimic these familiar paper techniques.

Prototype inheritance

Once we've made the duplicate, however, we have *two* copies of the common information. If that information is wrong, or if it's superseded someday, we'll need to correct it twice: in the original and in the copy.

Instead of *duplicating* a note and then editing the copy, we can tell Tinderbox to make a new note "just like" another note, with the exception of those attributes we want to change. The existing note becomes a model or *prototype*.

If a note has a prototype, Tinderbox looks first at the note itself for any information Tinderbox needs. If that information isn't explicitly specified for that note, Tinderbox examines the note's prototype. If Tinderbox doesn't find the information in the prototype, then it continues to look for the prototype's own prototype. In the end, if value still isn't specified, Tinderbox uses the attribute's default value.

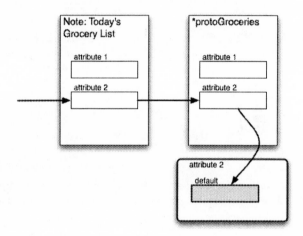

Figure 14. If a note has a prototype, it inherits values from the prototype. If no value is specified in either the note or its prototype(s), Tinderbox uses the default value.

Observe that inheritance applies only to attributes of a note to which no specific value has been assigned. Suppose a prototype **protoOfficial** is green, and a newly created note, **Thomas Hudson**, uses **protoOfficial** as its prototype. The note **Thomas Hudson** will be green. If we change **protoOfficial**'s color to blue, **Hudson** will turn blue as well; it inherits the color. But if we change Hudson to red, further changes to the color of **protoOfficial** won't change Hudson's color.

Any note can serve as a prototype for other notes. A special attribute, CanBePrototype, tells Tinderbox that a note expects to serve as a prototype; notes marked CanBePrototype appear in the popup Prototype menu. But, even if a note is not included on this menu, or if it is later removed from the menu, notes can use it as a prototype.

> Detail: Prototypes are implemented as a special link that connects the prototype to its instances. Prototype links are usually drawn in a distinctive color; many Tinderbox users prefer to make Prototype links invisible.

Every note has, at most, one prototype. But prototypes can inherit from their own prototypes, creating inheritance chains.

> Detail: CanBePrototype is among the select list of attributes that are *not* inherited. If CanBePrototype were inherited normally, then all notes that used a prototype would themselves be marked as potential prototypes.

Inheritance and Dependence

Inheritance creates a dependence between two notes. Changing the value of a prototype's attribute changes the value of all of its instances, *unless those instances have already established their own, independent value.*

This sort of dependence helps organize work and avoids unwanted duplication of information. Duplicate information is inconvenient, of course, because you have to type it over and over. Prototypes save unnecessary typing. More important, though, duplicate information is difficult to revise and update. Suppose William Perkins' phone number changes, and I need to update my notes. If two independent notes contain Perkins' phone number, I need to change it in two places. If I overlook one of those places, I might later find the obsolete phone number. Just as bad, I might later find *both* phone numbers; which do I choose? If I revise the number in several places, but mistype the number in one place but not the other, I find myself in much the same pickle.

> **Note**: Over time, some errors naturally accumulate
> in your notes. Avoiding mistakes, and making errors
> evident, is always desirable. If *all* Perkins' phone
> numbers are incorrect, I'll discover the problem
> when next I call Perkins. If *some* are right and others
> wrong, I may not discover the problem for months.
> Then, I will naturally correct the error, but the same
> problem might well crop up again in other notes.
>
> Inaccurate or "dirty" information leads us to distrust
> our notes. Distrust tempts us to begin to keep some
> information elsewhere, because the notes can't be
> trusted, and this worsens the problem. Keeping
> your information clean is important not only for using
> that information but also for your continued
> confidence in the notes as a whole.

Prototypes let us enter and revise information in one place – in the prototype – and share that information among many notes. This sharing, incidentally, has almost no cost, because Tinderbox implements inheritance very efficiently.

Occasionally, propagation of changes is neither intended or desired. At times, you may want to create completely independent notes, perhaps duplicating a note and then editing it without creating any inheritance relationship. If you want two notes, for example, to have similar appearance but the notes are otherwise unrelated, copying and pasting makes more sense than using prototypes.

Using Inheritance

One common Tinderbox task is the *daybook* – a collection of notes about things that happen during the day, a sort of laboratory notebook for everyday business life. My daybook records things I might want to remember later – decisions I made, where I put things, when I mailed a check or placed an order.

Let us suppose that I often want to jot down records of phone conversations connected with my research project, not as a formal phone log but simply as an aide-mémoire. I could simply make plain old notes after each call, but instead I define a prototype note, **protoCall**, which looks a little like the old-fashioned pink phone message notes (Figure 15).

The prototype is set up with relevant key attributes. This saves time and focuses attention after a phone call on the message, rather than on Tinderbox mechanics. The note is pink in the map, and when its text window is open its distinctive background color and typeface remind me instantly that telephone notes are not purchase orders or memoranda. Months or years from now, when a telephone note appears in a search result, I'll be able to see what it is at a glance.

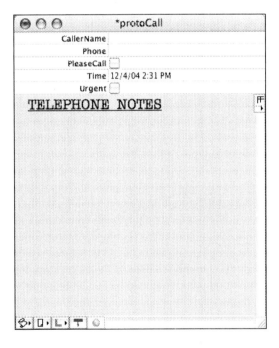

Figure 15. A prototype for recording notes about telephone calls.

Over time, I might add more prototypes to my daybook. One represents purchases, another product ideas or new software concepts. Each prototype can have its own key attributes and its own distinctive appearance.

Prototypes gain additional power because they are easy to extend. Suppose, for example, that I notice myself making essentially the same note, time and again:

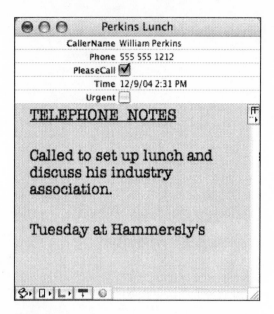

Figure 16. If Perkins calls almost every month to arrange lunch, this message may itself be a useful prototype.

Perkins and I have lunch frequently, roughly once a month. It's usually on Tuesday. But I can't simply schedule a monthly lunch on my calendar; sometimes he's out of town, sometimes I'm away, and sometimes we'll decide to have dinner instead.

I can easily select one of these messages and click its **Can be a prototype** checkbox. Now, "Perkins Lunch" appears on the prototype menu. When Perkins calls, I can instantly create a new note modeled after Perkins Lunch. The phone number and caller will be automatically filled in because it is inherited from the prototype, but of course I can change these if, for example, Perkins is working this week from his London office. The "usual" text is entered automatically, but I can extend or change it as needed.

Refactoring Key Attributes

When several different notes share a common set of key attributes, this suggests that the notes possess a common structure. New notes might be able to take advantage of that structure, saving time while giving you better structure and improved data integrity.

In this case, we create a prototype note to establish a logical connection from the new note to the prototype. This connection tells Tinderbox that the new note is exactly like its prototype, except for differences you've explicitly changed. The prototype also helps link related notes.

>   Note: A few aspects of notes are *intrinsic* to the
>   note, and never inherited. For example, every note
>   has its own map location, so Xpos and Ypos are
>   never inherited. Similarly, each note's Created time
>   is defined when it is created and its Modified time is
>   defined when it is changed Neither will be inherited
>   from the prototype.

A common case appears when a group of notes all use the same Key Attributes. A shared set of key attributes often suggests that all the notes are members of a single class or type of note:

- Key attributes usually represent the distinctive patterns of data associated with a class of note
- Lists of key attributes can be tedious to set up, so inheriting key attributes can save a substantial amount of time

When a family of notes shares a set of key attributes, it is often useful to create a new prototype, set its key attributes appropriately, and then to use it as the prototype for each note. But existing notes may already have their own set of key attributes. You'll want to remove those key attributes so the notes all inherit their key attributes from the prototype.

To reset the value of an attribute to the default:

1) Open the Quick Stamp palette (cmd-1)
2) Select the attribute you want to reset from the attributes popup menu
3) Select the note(s) of interest in any view window
4) Press the **use default** button

Actions can also restore a default value:

Color=; Price=; Quantity=;

restores the default values of Color, Price, and Quantity.

Managing Prototypes

A prototype is simply a note; in principle, any note can be a prototype. (The attribute CanBePrototype controls whether a prototype appears in the prototype menu, but even notes for which CanBePrototype is false may serve as prototypes if you wish.)

Some Tinderbox users prefer to reserve prototypes to act only as exemplars. Others choose actual notes to serve as prototypes, notes that are actively used in the document. Some prefer to make lots of prototypes soon after creating a new document, others add prototypes gradually as they discover a need.

> Note: People familiar with object-oriented computer programming are accustomed to defining classes before using them, and so it seems natural to define prototypes before making any notes.
>
> Those who have taught object-oriented programming, however, consistently find that students are confused by the distinction between classes and instances. People who aren't expert programmers often prefer to get on with the work rather than creating lots of abstract classes.
>
> Prototype inheritance blurs the distinction between class and instance, because any instance can define a new class. Every note can be a prototype, every note can use a prototype, and you can change prototypes whenever you like.

When creating notes that are intended to serve as prototypes, it is often useful to adopt a special naming convention, giving prototypes names like •PurchaseOrder or protoContract. Starting prototype names with a bullet or other symbol helps agents and containers sort all the prototypes together, and helps distinguish prototypes in the Find and Locate views.

Note: Early Tinderbox users often used asterisks to distinguish prototype names, e.g. *protoContact. As more recent versions of Tinderbox introduced arithmetic expressions, the use of asterisks can lead to confusion and is no longer recommended.

Hiding Prototype Links

In Map views, prototypes are linked to the notes that use them; Tinderbox prototypes use links to keep notes and prototypes connected. Often, prototype links make maps seem complicated; if prototype links begin to obscure more meaningful relationships, simply hide them. In the Link Types panel of the attributes palette, select the **prototype** link type and uncheck the checkbox that makes prototype links **visible** (Figure 17).

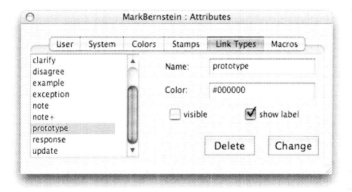

Figure 17. Hiding link types can help clarify maps.

Refactoring Information to Prototypes

As a project proceeds, you will frequently notice new patterns and regularities in your notes. Often, the first sign of these patterns is redundancy or repetition; you find yourself typing the same information several times. We've just addressed one example of this phenomenon with respect to Key Attributes (page 62), but whenever we find a quantity of similar notes, we're likely to discover opportunities to extract prototypes by refactoring shared information.

Let's revisit our digital camera procurement project from Chapter 1. Our goal was to review current technologies and products with an eye to ultimately selecting the best match for our needs. To begin, we might read some recent product reviews from industry journals, both to learn about specific offerings and to get a better picture of the product space. In the process, we create a number of notes about specific products:

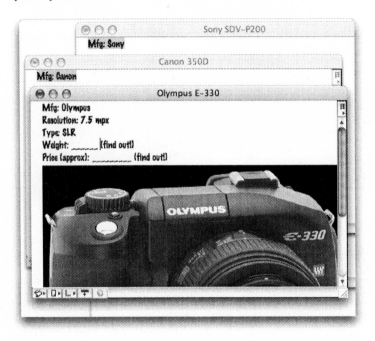

Figure 18. Early information gathering collects many unstructured notes. Later, refactoring common elements to prototypes can save typing and improve accuracy, consistency, and correctability.

Recall that our early gathering work was not done in order that we might learn about specific cameras but rather that we might learn what we will need to know in order to reach an informed decision – what factors to take into account, and what information sources we can use to gather reliable facts and opinion. We don't, at this point, know how we'll organize and classify the cameras, and any early attempt to predetermine this classification (e.g. by assembling a preliminary outline) might prejudice our decision.

In time, some regularities will emerge, and we will eventually choose a list of base information we want to gather about every camera. Perhaps these include its manufacturer, model number, resolution, and price. We can refactor this information into attributes, creating a prototype **protoCamera** that automatically sets the key attributes that cameras will share.

Figure 19. As we learn more about the problem space, we extract common elements shared by all cameras (like their key attributes) to a shared prototype.

If we require a very detailed and thorough survey, gathering information about hundreds of cameras, we might well create several prototypes that describe general classes or categories of camera. These additional prototypes inherit most of their properties from the core Camera prototype, but can add additional information. The more specific prototypes can automatically fill in some attributes by supplying default values we typically expect. Of course, some models might differ from our expectations, and individual cameras simply override the prototype's default value.

Keep in mind that *any* note can serve as a prototype. Many new products are best described as updates to a familiar product; we say, "this camera shares all the features with last year's model, but includes a higher-resolution sensor and new software at a lower price." We can easily express this relationship by making the old model serve as a prototype for the new model.

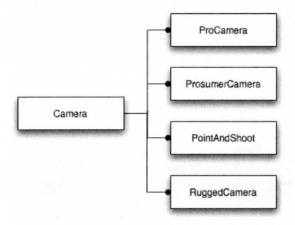

Figure 20. Additional prototypes can add information about new cameras while setting default values.

Multiple layers of inheritance can save typing, and at the same time concentrate shared information in one place. If you write the manufacturer's phone number in the notes on each camera, then a new phone number might require an update to many different notes. If the phone number is inherited from the prototype, the change can be entered in one place and inherited by all the notes that use it.

Inheritance and Linking

Inheritance competes with conventional links; we can *inherit* information from a prototype or *link to* information in a separate note. Extending the previous example of information about camera manufacturers, we might envision several notemaking strategies:

- Manufacturer information could be recorded with each camera
- Manufacturer information could be recorded in prototypes for each manufacturer, and inherited by individual cameras

- Manufacturer information could be recorded in separate notes, and those notes could be linked to notes about individual cameras.

Each approach has distinct advantages and weaknesses. Recording vendor information with each camera is convenient and flexible, but can entail redundant data that may prove hard to maintain. Inheritance cleanly isolates shared data, but is potentially complex and can be excessively rigid. Observe especially that a note can have no more than one prototype; if we have already adopted the prototype categories of Figure 20 and add a layer of vendor prototypes, we will have a very long prototype list indeed, with names like `protoCameraPointAndShootSony`. As the prototype tree becomes bushy, adding new classes – especially new classes near the root of the tree – comes to entail adding an entire new set of subclasses. If our needs change, reorganizing a complex prototype hierarchy can be arduous.

Linking cameras to vendors provides less formal leverage – we can't automatically fill out forms by making a link – but is in other ways more flexible than inheritance. We can add manufacturer links to some cameras where this information is pertinent, but not to others where its utility is doubtful. If one camera is available from two vendors, we can express this with two links but not with two prototypes, as a note can have only one prototype. It's easy to add more links, or to define new kinds of links, or to delete links you no longer need – much easier than revising a tangled inheritance tree.

Prototypes and Classes

In practice, Tinderbox prototypes define *ad hoc* classes of notes. The prototype Camera and the prototypes that inherit from it define a set of notes about specific cameras. We might well have other kinds of notes, many of which will have their own prototypes.

- Manufacturer
- Sources of information
- Field Test Reports
- User Requirements

Each kind of note may have different key attributes, and may also fit in distinct ways into your workflow. Notes about information sources – web sites, product reviews, industry newsletter – will form a list of references to give your recommendations weight, and also provide a vital resource if you need to defend your report from rivals and critics. You'll want to record them and manage them differently, for example, than you'll manage the survey results and memos that generate your notes about user requirements.

It is often useful to use distinctive color schemes or borders to distinguish different classes of note. By making the different kinds of notes more visually apparent, you can quickly notice anomalies and mistakes.

Automatically Selecting Prototypes

Tinderbox prototypes are a powerful tool for capturing and organizing knowledge. Prototypes often represent what kind of information a note contains – whether a note represents a book you might need to cite, a task you need to do, or a business contact who might become a customer.

Often, you'll create some notes and discover later that they should share the same prototype. Still later, you might find that some of these notes should share a more specific prototype: a note might first become a Reference and later a JournalReference or an AssignedReading to be distributed to your students. The process of discovering and refining prototypes is part of incremental formalization.

If it's hard to assign or change prototypes, people tend to avoid prototype information entirely. What if something is miscategorized? Fear of premature commitment can overwhelm other considerations, leading people to call everything "a note" and leave it at that.

To avoid this, Tinderbox makes it very easy to change the prototype of a note: just **Rename** the note and choose the new prototype. (Changing the prototype might hide some key attributes but it won't erase information that's already part of the note, so changing the prototype isn't a hazardous task.)

If you need to change the prototype of a lot of notes, consider using a power tool.

- You can make a **stamp** that sets the prototype of the selected note; this is handy for prototypes you need frequently
- A **quickstamp** for setting the prototype gives you the power of a stamp without the overhead. It's ideal when you need to set a big batch of prototypes today, but don't expect to need the stamp tomorrow.
- Having trouble locating the notes whose prototype you want to change? Remember that the **Find** window is a full-fledged view, and works with stamp and Quickstamp exactly like map and outline windows do.
- If you find yourself using **Find** to set a prototype, you might consider creating an agent that permanently looks for notes that fit your search criteria and sets the Prototype automatically.

The most common and powerful way to automate prototypes is to use the **context** of a note to deduce what sort of note it is. For example:

- If our document contains some Projects, each of which holds one or more Tasks, then the Project's OnAdd action can set the prototype. Whenever a note is added to a Project, it becomes a Task.
- If our document has an Adornment labeled "Things To Finish Today Without Fail", we might set the adornment's action to assign the prototype UrgentTask.
- We might also use a Tinderbox rule to set the prototype. For example, if a Task mentions "weblog" in the text, you might automatically change the prototype from Task to the more specific ComputerTask.

6. Emergent Structure

Emergent Structure

Tinderbox documents are organic, and many are *volatile,* changing frequently as you add and organize information. As your understanding grows, and as your needs change, you are bound to uncover new ways of working and new aspects of your work that you wish to record. In particular, some facets that you originally captured only occasionally and informally will often take on greater importance. Over time, you may create new attributes to describe them and new agents and actions to take advantage of those attributes. This entire process is the discovery of *emergent structure.*

Let's consider a simple, practical example. One day, in the midst of a long and busy meeting, your boss might delegate a small but open-ended research task.

> *Should we update the cellular phone plan for our sales group? Are we using the right technology? Look into it and make sure we're on the right track.*

Now, this is a small task, not a major assignment, but it requires effort and intelligence over time – that is to say, it takes work: gathering information from a variety of sources, comparing services from different vendors. Perhaps we should meet with some members of the sales group in order to clarify their needs. We might contact colleagues for their experiences, or consult industry observers and/or specialists.

A simple collection of Tinderbox notes takes only a moment to set up – hardly longer than opening a new word processing document or grabbing a fresh legal pad from the supply cabinet. Nonetheless, Tinderbox notes provide some immediate, tangible advantages:

- Since they're electronic, Tinderbox notes are easy to archive. There's less risk of lost time because notes were left in the car, or (worse) on the airplane
- Tinderbox notes are easily shared with colleagues and collaborators. Using the Tinderbox demonstration version, colleagues can *read* notes even if they don't yet own Tinderbox.
- Tinderbox lets you quickly and easily share information through the Web, while giving you complete control over its contents and appearance
- Much business information today arrives in electronic form, either in email or through Web pages. I can drag this information right into Tinderbox. Similarly, when I want to share a single note, I can easily copy it into an email message.
- Tinderbox features extremely fast search; if I misplace a fact, I can easily track it down.
- Tinderbox maps make good visual aids for meetings – flexible enough to allow last-minute changes and additions, but also clear and engaging for maximum impact.

After comparing six or eight telephone vendors, you may reach a simple conclusion and wind up the project. But casually delegated tasks sometimes become long-range commitments, and you might acquire a lasting responsibility to monitor the area and to make sure the enterprise stays abreast of changing technologies – and of changing demands from the sales team. New vendors will enter the marketplace, new products will emerge, price points will change. Over time, you may find articles and news stories that explore related business issues, that report on the decisions our competitors have made, that predict future trends or point out possible errors we want to avoid. All of this, in time, will find its way into your Tinderbox notes.

As you learn more about the industry, the vendors, and about your own enterprise's needs, though, you will doubtless learn how to organize this growing collection of notes more effectively. You might, for example, come to value some trusted analysts and columnists. At first, these sources might have merely been noted occasionally and inconsistently in the text.

> *Read a column by Julie Smithson, comparing new messaging technologies recently deployed in Japan. She reports that...*

Later, we might systematically emphasize the provenance as one of the key facts about the piece.

> **Messaging Spreads In Finland**
> *source: The Smithson Report*
> *Julie Smithson interviews J. Tollefsen on increasing use of techniques originally deployed in Japan...*

Now, agents can search for patterns like "source: The Smithson Report" to list all notes from this source. Still later, we might define an attribute called "source" to represent this information even more explicitly; the old agent can help us fill in the value automatically in older notes.

> Query: Text(source: The Smithson Report)
> Action: source="The Smithson Report"

Uncovering Structure

Moving critical information from your memory into Tinderbox text, and from unstructured text into attributes, is often the key to more effective research and more cogent analysis. This process may be gradual; you don't need to formalize immediately or completely. Indeed, premature formalization is often mere procrastination. Students, for example, are often tempted at the outset of a course into spending many hours carefully arranging their supplies, adorning their notebooks, and preparing to make and analyze their course notes. But gradually extracting detail into explicit form can be powerful and rewarding, helping you to understand the information that you already know and to identify gaps in your knowledge.

We often keep lists of things we want to find out, but we're constantly learning new facts and discovering new concepts. Until you write it down (Chapter 1), you may not realize what you've learned.

Setting down and handling new information helps you discover what matters, and why. Implicit knowledge becomes visible and explicit, implicit desires and unmet needs become action items – or things you consider and put aside. You don't need to set out to make decisions; simply reviewing your lists or cleaning your databank will help you know what you need and what you really want.

Finally, it's important to respect how complex and deeply linked the world can be. Everything *is* intertwingled [21]. It's a complex world, filled with tangled relationships and subtle dependences. Whether you're trying to plan how to pull together the information for your taxes or to decide whom to invite to your wedding, you're bound to discover complications you'd never anticipated.

Resolutions Reconsidered

When starting a new project or starting a new year (or a new job), it's tempting to try to get the organization exactly right. *This time,* we tell ourselves, *we'll get it all down, and we'll get it right the first time.* We'll define the structure, the filing system, the procedure, and we'll follow it. Our subordinates and collaborators will follow it, too. Or else.

This philosophy underlies a host of products and knowledge management methodologies we call "formal tools" when we're being formal, or "New Year's Resolution tools" when we're not. These are the sorts of organizers that encourage you to get everything wonderfully neat and tidy first, and then roll up your sleeves and get down to work. But, somehow, things always seem to get messier and messier over time. The promise of the neat (but empty) folders and the beautifully labeled (but unpopulated) database tables gradually evaporates under the press of work load and change.

As you learn, plans change – including your plans for learning, analyzing, and sharing your data.

When elaborate systems fail to meet their promise, blame follows. In team environments, we usually blame subordinates (for not following rules) or management (for not understanding the structure). When we're working alone, we blame our busy schedules and the unreasonable awkwardness of our tools. *It's not my fault this is turning into be a mess,* we reassure ourselves. *If the program were faster, or the user interface were better, or if I could only have brought that heavy laptop along with me, it would all have worked.*

Usually, the fault lies not the user interface, but in the inevitable mismatch between the natural and volatile organization of our information and our initial preconceptions. The organization at the outset is never either complete or correct. However elaborately we have prepared our inboxes and labeled our bins, soon we'll find boundary cases. "Is this really 'urgent'?", we ask, "Or is it only "important'?" If we have separate bins for "customer requests" and "vendor issues", what happens when a vendor buys our product, or when we hire a customer as freelance consultant? The more complex the system, the more rapidly the friction of raw, unanticipated reality is likely to abrade it. And, soon, we discard the structures or we start to abuse them, to hedge them with mental reservations and procedural footnotes.

Tinderbox workspaces, on the other hand, often improve over time. Tinderbox encourages you to start small, to begin with the simplest thing that could possibly work [14], and to get on with the business of gathering information. Over time, Tinderbox makes it easy to gradually find and refine structure – and just as easy to put aside structure that didn't work out.

Informal Lists

Tinderbox makes it easy to make and organize spontaneous lists. You can make a note into a container instantly – just drag another note into it. It's easy, too, to move notes among containers. If you're not sure exactly where a note goes, you can use the Map view to arrange notes in tentative clusters.

Sometimes, you aren't sure whether you want a container or not.
Here, the *separator* can be a used to advantage.   A separator is just a
plain old note, but it's just used to mark a boundary.

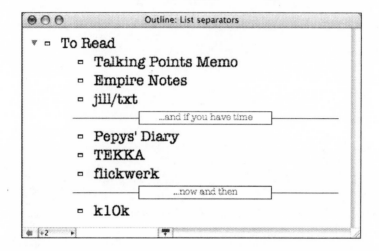

Figure 21. Separator notes indicate informal and fuzzy boundaries. Use
them when you suspect a category is emerging, but you aren't confident
it's quite clear or precisely right.

For example, I can easily keep a list of Web sites I check often, or
want to remind myself to check, or that someone had suggested I
review. Sometimes, especially after a good meeting, the backlog
becomes substantial: I've been offline for several days, so I've got to
catch up on my reading, I've promised a bunch of people I'd look at
sites they'd recommended, and I've got a bunch of research ideas or
marketing questions that need to be researched.

The first problem is just to get everything written down. *Any
Tinderbox system is better than just trying to remember.* The simplest
thing that could possibly work is, for this, just fine.

> **Tip:** When starting a new project, don't hesitate to
> make a fresh Tinderbox document and simply start
> taking notes. Perhaps you're not sure how things
> should be organized, or exactly what attributes
> you'll need. Don't worry; just go ahead and work.
> Once you learn more, you'll gain confidence and

insight – and those early notes will still be valuable.
You can always go back and edit them; you won't
be able to go back and reclaim time spent setting
up an elaborate system that turned out not to fit the
realities of your data.

The second problem is setting priorities; identifying key information and urgent actions, and sorting these from items that are less important or less pressing. Some things can't, or shouldn't, wait. Some, clearly, can be postponed; I may enjoy reading a bit of Pepys' Diary every day, but it was written centuries ago and it won't change if I put it off 'til tomorrow.

Some priorities are bound to be fluid: the item that hardly seemed urgent yesterday may be, this morning, a crying need. If, today, we put everything that's not an emergency into a container, will we even notice the items that, by tomorrow, may demand immediate attention? Containers can become barriers; things tucked neatly inside a container may escape notice, while things left lying atop our desk demand attention.

Separator notes serve as extremely lightweight containers. If containers are walls, separators are curtains. Often, separators are completely informal and *ad hoc*: this kind of separator is handy, for example, if a list is becoming too long to comprehend at a glance. In lieu of shortening the list or reorganizing the document, we can simply add some separators and rapidly partition or prioritize the list, hand-sorting it into a few categories.

- Assigning tasks among team members and subordinates
- Identifying emergency, urgent, and less urgent action items
- Allocating resources (or facilities) to projects
- Determining the most critical features of a planned purchase, a new hire, or a future project.

If you find yourself using separator notes frequently in a project, it may be worthwhile to define a special prototype for separators. This lets you make specifier notes more easily, and also encourages a little more elaboration in the document since a single prototype can enhance all the separators. I often choose a distinct font for separators by setting NameFont, and set a special color as well.

Tip: It's often best to choose a font, or a color, that
suggests *less* emphasis than normal notes carry.
Separators are apparatus and shouldn't call too
much attention to themselves. Legible script fonts,
or lightweight typewriter fonts, are often ideal.

If you're sharing your notes on the Web, you probably won't want to export the separators; just set `HTMLDontExport` to true, or open the HTML View window for the separator prototype and turn off **Export as page**.

In time, you may find that the separators represent valuable categories that should really be containers. That's easy to fix; just create a container (or perhaps the former separator will do!) and drag the notes under the separator into it. If you find yourself doing this frequently, there's even a menu item – **Demote Younger Siblings** in the Note menu moves all the notes following the current note inside it.

Over time, old and oft-used separators tend to become containers. But many separators last only a short time; use them for their immediate task and, if they no longer seem useful, delete them.

Windows for Special Containers

It often saves time and nuisance to keep separate windows open for viewing the contents of a few special containers. For example, research notes often need a container that represents a list of sources – books, articles, Web sites. We might require this information, eventually, for a bibliography or a list of references, but even if that's not a factor it's valuable to know how to find a source again. You have the information ready-to-hand; why not preserve it?

The container that holds the source list can take care of some clerical tasks automatically, too. Often, most of the notes created inside a container will share the same prototype, so letting the container assign the prototype automatically saves effort. The container can also keep notes alphabetized, or sorted by date or by priority.

Of course, most of the time you don't want to be looking at a long list of references. You want to view your work, not the records you're saving just in case they might prove useful. It makes sense, then, to tuck all the references for a project into a separate container, and to keep a separate window open to this list. If you select an individual reference from the container and choose **New Outline View** from the Views menu, Tinderbox will open a new window, listing the contents of the reference container. You can resize this window, perhaps making a tall, narrow window at the edge of your screen

- Your references will be handy, so you won't be tempted to postpone creating a reference note. Just select the references window from the Windows menu, press Return, and you're ready to make a new note.
- Your reference list will also be readily available as a link target. Links can be a terrific shorthand for keeping notes attached to their source. Knowing where a note came from can save you hours someday – but only if it's so easy to make the link that you aren't tempted to skip it because the connection is obvious and you're in a rush.

> Tip: If worst comes to worst, other Tinderbox metadata can help you reestablish lost connections. Tinderbox always records the creation date of every note, and this date never changes. Once you know that you made a note on, say, January 16, you can check your reference list for sources you consulted around that day.

- If screen space is tight, you can keep the Reference window near the edge of the screen, and let your main windows overlap its edges as needed. As long as some part of the window is visible, you'll be able to select it easily with the mouse. If screen space is very short, you can always maximize your main work view.
- If you'd like to include sources in different maps, just select the source in the reference container and make an alias. Then drag the alias into the map.

> Tip: Tinderbox often provides several good ways to do things, and this is no exception. Instead of putting all the sources in a reference container, you might prefer to scatter them throughout a document. That's no problem! You'll almost certainly want to create a prototype for references.

Experimental Structure: Maps and Spatial Hypertext

The Tinderbox Map View is often a convenient way to experiment with structure. Maps let you try out a structure that seems to be emerging from the data. If the new organization seems useful, the map provides an easy way to work with it and to explain it to others. Just as important, the map may reveal quickly that the proposed organization is a dead end, or that a different approach will prove better.

Consider a small work team – perhaps a task force at work, or a university research group, or even a law school study group. Over the course of time, the group will engage a variety of topics and need to undertake a number of projects. Some will be assigned to individuals, others will require collaboration. Some will be delivered on time, others will be late. Some desirable tasks may be deferred because the team doesn't have time to undertake them at once. Others may be delayed because they must wait upon events, or because they require facilities or information that will only become available later.

Keeping tabs on all this activity can be a challenge. Capable software exists for planning and tracking more complex projects. In managing a construction site or a highway project, for example, hundreds of workers and dozens of vendors must be coordinated every day. But the planning tools for this kind of project management are seldom a good fit for small teams. They expect deadlines to be rigid (like contracts) and dependencies to be clear and well defined. You simply can't start the roof until the walls are in place. Small-team work often isn't like that: you might *prefer* to have Henderson's report in hand before the client presentation, or it might be *better* to write the grant proposal after the current results are completely analyzed, but these dependencies are soft. They can be avoided if necessary. Large projects require rigid constraints, but smaller projects often benefit from complex and subtle tradeoffs.

How can we represent and discuss these tradeoffs? First, of course, we need to write everything down. We make a note for each task, giving each a concise descriptive title. That alone might be sufficient; it's bound to be better than trying to remember what everyone is supposed to be doing!

Next, we can roughly arrange tasks on the map. Urgent tasks can be grouped in one place. Completed tasks are dragged elsewhere, or filed away in a container for later reference. Less urgent tasks can be grouped in their own location. Within these groups, related notes can easily be clustered together.

Next, we can make visible some of the most relevant properties of each note, using Tinderbox's wide array of system attributes. Some of the properties we can use include:

```
Color
Color2 (the note's secondary color)
Pattern (e.g. gradient, diagonal or lines)
Border
BorderColor
Height
Width
NameFont
NameBold
NameColor
```

We might begin very informally, perhaps by setting the color of a few notable tasks. Some properties of the work may demand particular attention; perhaps we will identify tasks with a rigid deadline by giving them a broad border. Tasks that are assigned to an individual or subcommittee might be distinguished by using a distinctive gradient, while unassigned tasks continue to use a solid color.

Just as important, we may discover that our initial representation is wrong. Perhaps we need to show the *kind* of task more prominently? We can use Border Color for that, instead of representing deadlines with red borders. Urgent tasks might now be shown with a distinctive font, or in bold face. Alternatively, agents or rules could modify each title to reflect its status:

```
Name=$ProjectName+": ("+$Status+")"
```

In time, these visual conventions become a useful shorthand for reasoning about the project and its component parts. The map can serve both as a management and coordination tool and as a focus for discussion in the group.

As you gain confidence in the representation's utility, connections between data and visual properties might be automated with prototypes, rules, and agents. If urgent items have red borders, for example, an agent could identify suitable items and change their border color.

Meta Space

Reserve a place in your repository for meta notes – notes about your notes, your process for making and analyzing them, and your reflections on them.

For example, you might reserve a few pages in the front of your paper notebooks and journals for front matter, such as a thematic index or overview, or a summary. This could be a simple chronological précis:

> 11: Vienna. Ringstrasse trams. Museums. More
> museums. Long walks. Gruner Veltiner.

> 16: Salzburg. More museums. Unexpected concert.
> Lack of evening wear proves no obstacle.

> 19: Munich. Meeting Dr. H. at the Alte
> Pinakothek.

Or, you might instead (or in addition) summarize recurrent themes:

> Airplanes, bane of existence: 17, 19, 31-3

> Bad manners, regretted: 42

> Closed

Museums, for repairs: 3, 4, 18

Stores, for the afternoon: 7, 18

Restaurants, for the month: 15, 27

Dr. H: 26, 37

Meta spaces in Tinderbox can easily be set aside by convention – for example, you might keep a cluster of meta notes in the upper right-hand corner, or place a container for meta notes at the top of your outline. If using a meta container, consider keeping a small window open to it all the time, making it even easier to locate when you're in a hurry.

Most often, meta spaces are marked off with adornments.

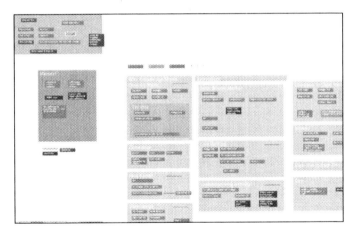

Figure 22. Tinderbox meeting notes, with two meta spaces at the left edge, indicated by adornments.

Here, we have two meta spaces at the left edge of a large collection of meeting notes. (The complete map continues several feet to the right.) One meta space collects notes about the notetaking process. As the first session of the meeting began, it became clear that capturing each speaker's name and contact information was a priority – especially since no printed proceedings were available; each speaker's information is contained in a note and marked off with a special turquoise color. Similarly, it soon seemed desirable to separate the speakers' positions from the lively discussions that followed: notes on presentations were made in coral while questions and commentary were noted in dark red. Finally, a second meta category called "memes" collects common themes among several sessions.

Meta space is an example of the ability of spatial hypertext to represent important but informal concepts quickly and without interrupting your thinking. Cornell note style is a related scheme for using different parts of a page for different kinds of notes.

Separating notes about process from notes about substance, while valuing both, helps retain focus while preserving space for complete consideration of all facets and alternatives.

7. Agents

Ephemeral Searches

Tinderbox excels at finding things.

Because Tinderbox offers you lots of ways to organize your notes, you're less likely to misplace old notes, or to forget where you've been writing. Maps provide spatial cues; though the placement of a note in a map may be arbitrary, its location with respect to other notes and to landmarks like adornments helps you remember where things are.

> When searching to relocate information they have seen before, people often use spatial cues that might seem irrelevant, and that they themselves are surprised they remember. When checking a striking passage in a novel, for example, it's not uncommon for people to find they remember approximately where the passage fell on the page. When searching for a lost memo or a missing book, people may remember aspects of layout and color, even if it is several months or years since they last saw the document.

Outlines provide a different kind of cue. By breaking long lists into small and specific components, outlines situate things more precisely, putting them where they belong – and where you expect to find them later.

Sometimes, you might forget where you put a note. Or, you may need to find a note in an unexpected context. The Tinderbox Find palette offers some powerful features that are sometimes overlooked.

First, remember that you can search for the patterns in the note name and text, or search specifically in either. You can also search the contents of any user attribute. Don't limit yourself to searching in Name and Text attributes.

Hint: In documents that depend heavily on lots of
attributes, it's easy to forget that searching Name
and Text may not locate the notes you're seeking.
For example, if your bibliographic notes have
separate attributes for author names, those names
might not appear in the text at all.

Figure 23. The Find palette in action. Tinderbox begins to locate notes as
soon as you begin typing.

While simple searches are by far the most common and
straightforward, you can use the Find window to search for regular
expressions with wildcards. For example, the character '.' will match
any single character. A full discussion of regular expressions will be
found below (page 95).

Note that many punctuation characters have special meanings when
searching, and so if you want to search for punctuation you must
precede these characters by a backslash '\'.

Not.	Matches "Note" and "Notify"
Not\.	Matches "Not."

The Find palette is a full-fledged Tinderbox view; you can use the Find window much as you use a map or outline.

- Select any note and press the space bar to open its text window
- Select any note and press Enter to rename it, or to edit its properties
- Select a note and choose New Outline View from the Views menu to locate that note in the document hierarchy
- Select a note and choose Get Info... from Note menu to see the note's word count and other useful statistics

You can also link to notes in the Find menu, just as you would link to notes in other Tinderbox views. This can make Find a particularly useful adjunct when writing. For example, when writing a weblog post you can easily locate previous posts that mention a topic or a person, review them for relevance, and then rapidly draw text links from the new essay to earlier postings.

Persistent Searches

Tinderbox agents are persistent search queries. Like the Find window, they scan your Tinderbox document, seeking a specific text pattern in each note and identifying notes that match the pattern. But unlike the Find window, agents remain active in your documents indefinitely. Agents are smart containers; they hold aliases to all the items that currently match their query.

Agents are notes. Like other Tinderbox notes, each agent has attributes that describe the agent's appearance and behavior. Agents have a Name and a Text window, just like other containers, and they can be viewed and exported.

> Hint: the "main page" of a weblog or news site is frequently an agent that scans the archives, identifies the latest additions, and sorts them so the latest news appears at the top of the page.

Agents are frequently useful for creating alternate views of a
container. For example, suppose we have a container of notes
regarding films we have seen. This container happens to be organized
in reverse chronological order, making it easy to review our most
recent notes and to add new notes.

> Films
>
> > The Two Towers
> >
> > Six Degrees of Freedom
> >
> > Bringing Up Baby
> >
> > Apocalypse Now
> >
> > … (many more films)

This may well be the most convenient way to add new notes, but
when we need to look up a specific film, we need to scan the entire
list. An agent can easily build an alphabetically-sorted index:

> **Agent: Films by Title**
> **Query: #inside(Films)**
> **Sort: Name**

This index is always up to date; Tinderbox agents run periodically
and update their contents automatically.

> Hint: you can toggle Update Agents Automatically
> (on the Tinderbox File menu) to enable or disable
> automatic agent updates. Very large documents
> with many complex agents can sometimes be slow
> – especially on older computers; if the agent
> updates interrupt your workflow, turn them off and
> update agents manually.

You may also reduce the priority of particularly
complex agents, so they will run less frequently.

Agent Actions

Like containers, agents may perform actions on notes that they locate.
Agent actions often set the values of attributes. For example:

    Query: Status=Urgent
    Action: Color=red;

This agent finds all notes that have been marked as Urgent and sets
their color. Any note that becomes Urgent will be red – and will
remain red until some other action changes the color.

Agents can be powerful tools to help discover structure in your notes.
For example, it is easy to build agents that construct topical categories
of special interest.

    Agent: Elizabethan
    Query: Text(Shakespeare)|Text(Marlowe)|Text(Fletcher)
    Action: Drama = true; Status |= Exciting

Here, we collect all notes that mention three Elizabethan playwrights,
we mark these notes as concerning Drama, and if the notes do not
already have a Status, we set the notes' status to "Exciting".

Cooperating Agents

Tinderbox agents scan the document, to find new and modified notes
that match their criteria. Often, it's helpful to let agents use the work
that other agents have already done.

For example, let's suppose we have an agent that looks for notes
about XML and related technology, sorting them by date. It might
look something like this:

    Agent: XML Agent

Query: Text(XML | Xpath | Xlink | W3C)
Sort: Created (reverse)

Other agents can leverage this. For example:

Agent: Technical News
Query: Created>"today-3 days"&
       (#inside(XML Agent) | #inside(Web Services))

This agent looks for notes created recently that are already listed by some relevant agents.

Some agents – especially those that match complex patterns that might appear anywhere in the text of a large collection of notes – can be computationally expensive; rather than search for the same items repeatedly, it is simpler and faster to use multiple agents:

Agent: New Notes about Elizabethans
Query: #inside(Elizabethan)&Created<"today-3 days"

At other times, we might want to reuse the agent indirectly: the agent sets an attribute and another agent looks for that value.

Agent: Exciting Drama
Query: Drama=true & Status(Exciting)

Notice that **Exciting Drama** may not always find the same notes as **Elizabethan**. When **Elizabethan** finds a note, to be sure, it sets the Drama flag and the status. Later, Elizabethan might no longer catalog the note (perhaps because we rewrote the text and omitted the playwright's name) but the attributes retain their values, and **Exciting Drama** will continue to list the note.

Agents act whenever they find a note that meets their criteria, but the action is not undone if the note later ceases to meet the agent's criteria.

Tinderbox agents are updated in the order in which they appear in the document outline. When a new agent relies on another, it is usually more efficient to place the new agent after the agents on which it relies .

Actions, Rules, and Prototypes

Tinderbox gives you several ways to choose prototypes – or to let Tinderbox choose them for you. Because composing notes is difficult and consuming work, it's often desirable to let Tinderbox automatically choose a suitable prototype. Fortunately, the prototype you intend can often be deduced from the context of the note and from the work you've been doing.

For example, let's suppose that some of your notes are **Projects**, and that a Project contains notes that describe **Tasks** you want to do.

First, you can simply choose the appropriate prototype from the pop-up menu of prototypes. This can be especially nice if you have several different kinds of Tasks – Errands, PhoneCalls, TopicsForReflection.

> Since the prototype menu is arranged in outline order, it's easy to arrange your prototypes so your popup menu is grouped intelligently.

The initial choice of prototype defaults to the prototype you used for the last note you created. When you are making notes in rapid succession, those notes are often similar, and this initial choice is especially likely to be correct when you're in a hurry.

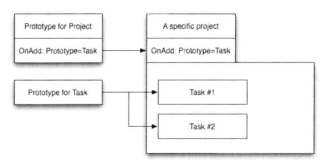

Figure 24. The prototypical Project asserts that the contents of any Project are initially Tasks – that is, their prototype is the prototypical Task. Users can later change the prototype if the note represents a task of a more specific kind.

The *OnAdd* action of the prototypical **Project**
container can assign the prototype **Task** to all
notes added to that project container. This
says, "A project normally contains Tasks", or
"Most of the things in a project are Tasks".
The user is free to select a different prototype
(e.g. **Errand** or **Conference Call** or **Press
Conference**) when appropriate; the OnAdd
action only applies when the note is added to
the container.

An *agent action* can automatically assign prototypes
based on the content and context of a note.
An agent can say, for example, that any task
that is not complete, not delegated, and
mentions groceries is a ShoppingErrand.

A *Rule* enforces a requirement. It's a constraint.
Where *OnAdd* means, "a note inside this
project is normally a Task", the corresponding
rule would mean, "Everything inside the
container must be a Task".

It is easy to build smart notebooks that can gradually adapt to the
way you'd like to work. Setting prototypes manually is not especially
arduous, so you can work effectively in a new document without
getting bogged down in automation. As you work, you can gradually
automate common cases to save time and typing. The prototypical
Project can say, "notes added here are Tasks"; the project for
DecemberDinnerParty can say, "notes added here are
ShoppingTasks", and the note about asking your sister in Seattle to
send a salmon can be automatically flagged by an agent as a
PhoneTask. You don't need this power for every project, but it's nice
to know it's there.

Regular Expressions

Agents can search for a specific string

    Name=Tinderbox

or for a string pattern

    Name(Tinder).

This second form locates all notes whose name contains the specified string. It will thus locate **The Tinderbox Way** and **Tinderbox Tips**, where the first form locates only the note named **Tinderbox**.

Sophisticated Tinderbox agents can be built using no more power than this. If you need more flexibility, Tinderbox patterns can be extremely elaborate and expressive.

WILDCARD CHARACTERS

The period character, ".", matches any single character.

The plus sign, "+", matches one or more occurrences of the expression that precedes it. So, that pattern

    !+

will match one or more exclamation points, and the pattern

    ...+

will match any string with at least three characters. An asterisk matches *zero* or more occurrences of whatever precedes it;

    10*

matches 1, 10, or 1000.

The "?" sign matches zero or one occurrence of whatever precedes it. You can even specify the minimum and maximum number of repetitions:

    Xa{2,4}Y

will match XaaY, XaaaY, or XaaaaY, but won't match XaaaaaaY.

RANGES

A set of characters to be matched may be enclosed in square brackets. For example,

[0123456789]

will match any digit. Ranges of consecutive characters can be written more concisely:

[0-9]

will match any digit, and

[A-Z][a-z]*

will match any capitalized word. Beginning a set with the character "^" matches everything *except* the set;

[A-Z][^0-9]

will match any capital letter provided it's not followed by a digit.

Several special sequences represent common sets of characters:

\w   any word character (including underscore)

\W   any non-word character

\<   the start of a word

\>   the end of a word

\s   any whitespace character

\d   any digit

\l   any lowercase letter

\u   any uppercase letter

ANCHORS

The special character "^" matches the beginning of the text or attribute being searched. When searching the **text** of a note, ^ matches the beginning of any paragraph in the note.

The special character "$" matches the end of the text or attribute being searched. When searching the **text** of a note, $ matches the end of any paragraph in the note.

THE \ CHARACTER

The backslash character "\" removes the special meaning from the character that follows it. Use "\\" to search for the backslash character itself.

PARENTHESIS

Grouping expressions in parenthesis determines the scope of wildcards. For example,

```
Name=(\u\l+)+
```
Would match "Rochester" and "SmallTalk".

In addition, when Tinderbox sees a parenthetical expression, it remembers the substring(s) that matched it and can use those substrings in actions. For example, the agent

```
Query: Text(^Color: (\w+)\b$)
Action: Color=$1
```
scans the document for any notes that contain paragraphs like this:

Color: red

If it finds any matching notes, the agent extracts the word that follows the string "Color: " and changes the note's color to match. Here, $1 stands for "whatever matched the first set of parenthesis", $2 for the second set, and so forth. $0 stands for the entire matched expression.

Hands On: Hotel Artemis

Managing information flow is always a critical challenge. Information arrives. Some information demands immediate response. Sometimes it suggests an emerging problem or a possible opportunity. Some merely bears watching. Much information is routine, fitting familiar patterns, but some is extraordinary and unexpected. In fact, the reason we select experienced people to manage business processes is often their ability to recognize routine patterns, to detect anomalies, and to find ways to satisfy extraordinary needs with ordinary processes.

In this scenario, we'll examine a hypothetical service management role. The same principles apply to a wide variety of workflows:

- an operations manager, receiving and analyzing trouble reports
- a magazine editor, tracking book reviews and reviewers
- a university professor, coordinating a half-dozen teaching assistants and perhaps 150 undergraduate students in a survey course
- an office manager, overseeing allocating shared facilities such as conference rooms and projectors, and also budgeting for future office needs
- a freelance journalist, managing an inventory of articles submitted to various magazines, story ideas and proposals in development, and new publishing markets to be explored

The salient characteristics of these areas include

- A steady stream of unstructured and partially-structured information, some of which needs to be retained for later study and action.

- The promise that better mastery of the information could generate substantial value.
- Responsibility (and authority) to ensure both that current problems are being handled appropriately and to devise plans and procedures to avoid unnecessary recurrence.

OVERVIEW

Priscilla Simmons is director of Guest Services at the Hotel Artemis, a luxury destination resort. A veteran hotelier, Priscilla brings a degree in Hotel Administration and some fifteen years of hospitality industry experience to her job. Her responsibilities are very broad, and though her management wants her to focus her attention on strategic planning, she's careful to keep a close eye on day-to-day operations. Every day, when she arrives at her desk at 7:30, she gets a cup of coffee and downloads priority email from a specialized mailbox named concierge-reports.

> **Tip:** One way to simplify your information-sorting tasks is to have your subordinates sort the information as they report it. Specialized mailboxes are a trivial expense – a few dollars per year. Because the concierge reports are always sent to a special mailbox, Priscilla can check them rapidly, without distraction. And, because only concierges and department managers file these reports, it is easy for Priscilla to arrange that they are routed to the appropriate address.

These reports describe every significant problem, complaint, or open task that arises between the hotel and a guest. Of course, most of Priscilla's managers can take care of most guest needs, answer most of their questions, and resolve most problems on the spot. But, if there's any likelihood that the guest will need to follow up, Priscilla wants to see a report in her mailbox before the end of shift.

- Reports keep the next shift abreast of developing situations. If a guest has a problem, that's bad; the Hotel doesn't want to make things worse by asking the guest to explain everything again, from the beginning, after every shift change.

- Reports let concierges and managers pool expertise and create a growing library of solutions. They also provide opportunities to let people work on each other's problems in time that might otherwise be idle.
- Reports help management make sure that front-line guest service personnel have the tools and staffing levels they need. By reviewing and analyzing reports, Priscilla can detect patterns of problems before they become chronic irritants.

Priscilla reads each report. Many are unremarkable, but if any aspect of the report catches her interest, she selects the text and drags it into a special Tinderbox document where she keeps interesting problems.

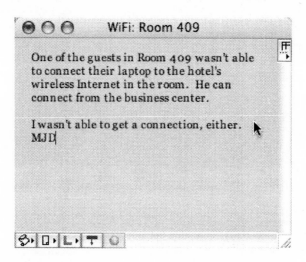

Figure 25 Priscilla selects text from the morning email and drags it into a dedicated Tinderbox file.

The morning's reports are always created inside a container called New Reports. This keeps them together for review, and lets the container's OnAdd action perform some basic housekeeping.

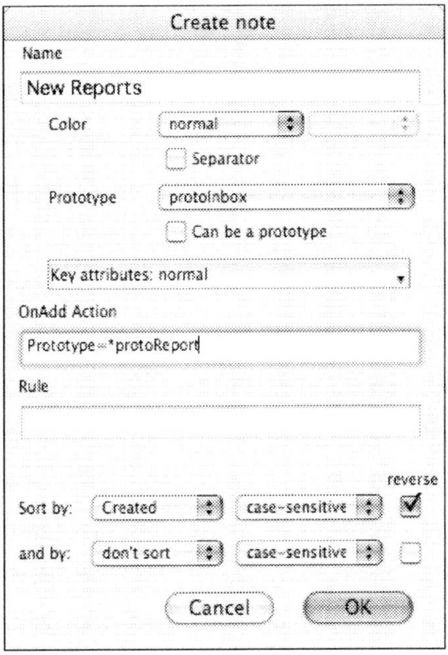

Figure 26. The New Reports container automatically sets the prototype of each newly created report. Reports are always sorted, too, with the most recent report at the top.

Reports are automatically assigned to the prototype **protoReport**, which sets up appropriate KeyAttributes. The color of the prototype *protoReport is an attention-getting bright red, so new reports are brightly colored; later, as reports are analyzed and filed, we may change their color to reflect their changing status.

SCALE

On a typical morning, Priscilla receives a few problem reports. Occasionally, the problem box is empty. On one memorable morning, she arrived to find over a dozen new reports. But a typical morning brings two or three problems to her attention, adding perhaps a thousand notes per year to her Tinderbox document.

This is the scale at which Tinderbox provides the greatest leverage. If Priscilla's staff reported only one exceptional problem a week, she probably wouldn't need Tinderbox at all. Whiteboards and paper files work well for individual items and short lists. Indeed, Priscilla could keep all the current problems in mind without difficulty. And, with only fifty items per year, we don't really need tools to analyze, track, or discover patterns; there's just not enough information there to reveal emergent structure.

Conversely, if Priscilla's inbox contained hundreds of reports on an average day, Tinderbox might not be the right tool for the job. With three hundred reports a day, we'd accumulate about 100,000 different notes in a year. That's too much information to keep in mind, obviously, but it's also too much to read and review. Tinderbox's visualization tools can't help much with 100,000 items; only a fraction could possibly be visible on the display at once. Tinderbox agents work continuously, and so even the fastest agents on the fastest computers will eventually become cumbersome. And, while Tinderbox uses a fast parser, the overhead of XML storage will itself, at some point, make loading and saving files intolerably slow. Data collections this large need to be rigidly structured if they are to be useful; an industrial database is probably the only viable option.

Tinderbox works best in the middle ground, with hundreds or thousands of notes.

CONTAINERS: PLANNING FOR GROWTH

At first, receiving a few new reports a day, Priscilla might simply keep all the reports in a single container. Over the course of a year, though, she'll accumulate several hundred reports, and so it makes sense to create a few separate containers to hold them.

Figure 27. Adding a few containers helps separate incoming notes that need special handling from those being saved for later analysis. Containers can automatically mark notes with time stamps and colors, reflecting their workflow status.

First, we make a separate container to hold prototypes. Keeping prototypes separate makes it easier to find them, and harder to change them accidentally.

Next, we create some containers to model our workflow – just as we might create paper files or inboxes if reports were filed on paper. Here, we have separate bins for:

- New issues which have just been reported
- Open issues, which Priscilla intends to follow or on which she might need to take action herself
- Problems that Priscilla particularly wants to revisit later
- Problems that have been solved, and which are being kept for reference and reuse
- Problems where the Hotel failed to find a completely satisfactory solution, but where nothing more can be done

These containers reflect the operation of Priscilla's department. New problems appear immediately in New Reports. Some are quickly resolved, and immediately move into the **Resolved** container. A few

are destined to fail, and move directly to the container of **Failed**
attempts. Some require immediate work, and these go in the Open
Issues folder.

USE WINDOWS EFFECTIVELY

It's often useful to keep several different windows open to different
parts of a Tinderbox document. At any moment, Priscilla's telephone
may bring her news about problems reports from **New Reports** and
Open Issues; keeping a window open on each of these containers
means that Priscilla doesn't need to navigate through an outline to
find them.

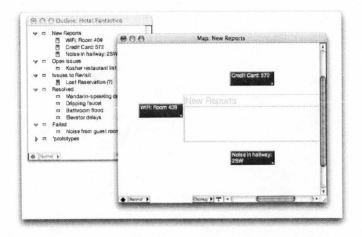

Figure 28. Keeping several windows open saves steps. This is especially
handy when email or phone calls may require access to particular
sections of the Tinderbox document. Remember that each view type has
its own strengths; don't rely exclusively on the same view.

Tinderbox beginners often try to do everything in one window, but it
can be more efficient to use several small windows, each tuned to its
own purpose.

REVISITING

Sometimes, we'd like to review a decision or series of events later – once the dust has settled and emotions have quieted. But it's easy, in the press of incoming issues, to forget what we once wanted to revisit.

We *could* schedule a formal review for a specific date, of course, using our calendar or PDA. But that's not precisely what we want. If we make an appointment, it's a commitment. That block of time is reserved, come what may.

That's not the level of commitment we require here. Suppose, for example, that Priscilla's inbox contains a disturbing report of a disagreeable contretemps concerning a reservation that was, apparently, either never made or which the Hotel somehow lost. There's nothing to be done now – whatever went wrong is past remedy – and the clerk involved is clearly upset. Priscilla would like to review this and see what lessons can be learned, but to pursue this at once might further inflame tempers. A fresh look next month would be appropriate.

But it doesn't matter at all, really, whether that fresh look happens on February 23rd or on the 24th. Scheduling events is costly – either you adhere to the schedule (and forgo other opportunities to use the time) or you constantly tinker with the schedule (which calls into question your commitment to any scheduled activity). Using your schedule for "revisiting" tasks is overkill.

Instead, we make a new Date attribute, **Revisit**, that marks the time when a note should be revisited. The container can set the time automatically:

Action: Revisit="today+3 weeks"; Color=dark magenta

Whenever we drop a note in the container, it's automatically tagged with a suggested revisit date.

We can now create an agent that lists notes we want to revisit (Figure 29).

CATEGORIES AND AGENTS

One of this morning's trouble reports strikes an ironic chord for Priscilla. Last night, one of her best people spent almost an hour, fruitlessly trying to help a guest connect to the Internet. First thing this morning, the guest called to say, "It works now!" They didn't teach Priscilla about wireless networking back in hotel school, but this sort of problem seems to appear up more and more frequently in Priscilla's inbox.

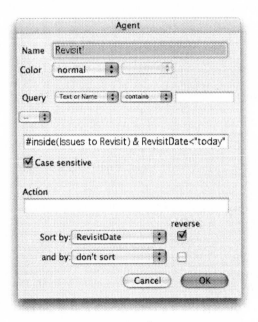

Figure 29. This agent finds issues that are ready to revisit, and sorts them with the most recent issues at the top of the list.

- Does the Hotel need to change its hiring or training practices, to increase the computer proficiency of the concierge staff?
- Should these issues be automatically dispatched, instead, to the Business Services department – a separate organization entirely?

- Should Priscilla consider a new staff position, a "computer concierge", who would be responsible for addressing problems like this?
- Or, should the Hotel build a relationship with outside contractors, much as they refer medical problems to outside physicians rather than employing doctors?

To answer questions like these, Priscilla needs more information. How often do challenging problems arise? Do guests *expect* the hotel to solve them, or do they see this as an extra service? Are problems increasing in frequency? In severity?

We can easily make an agent to keep an eye on computer-related problems. To begin, we'll simply watch for terms that suggest a computer issue:

> Agent: Computers
> Query: Text(internet)|Text(laptop)|Text(wireless)|Text(PC)

> Tip: Some of the terms you'll want to use for category agents will occur to you right away. To find others, scan some of your existing notes to find those you'd like the new agent to list. Most likely, you'll quickly discover some terms you missed. Also, review the agent's initial list for mistakes; some terms that seem specific to the problem might often occur in unrelated contexts. Problems with **wireless telephones** and reports initialed by Peter Cunningham (PC) might be misidentified.

> Tip: Simple agents are often best. It's tempting to make agents more and more elaborate, to get things exactly right. A few false hits, however, will cause no real difficulty in a study like this one. Your time is valuable, and complicated agents are slower and harder to understand and to improve.

Reviewing old notes, we might observe that some relevant problems don't have any of our keywords in the text. We want to be able to manually categorize a note, to tell Tinderbox that this note concerns a computer network issue.

Tinderbox provides several ways to manually categorize notes.

1) We might simply add a suitable keyword or phrase to the text. If we append the phrase "Category: internet" to incoming reports about network issues, the agent will see the phrase and collect the note.

2) We can define a new Boolean user attribute, *InternetProblem,* with a default value of False. By setting this true, we're asking the agent to collect it. The agent now looks for the attribute, too:

Query: InternetProblem=true | Text(internet) | .....

We might instead define a string user attribute, ProblemType, and add appropriate keywords there. The agent could look for "computer" in ProblemType as well as for keywords in the text. The same attribute could be used for other kinds of problems, and we can easily write several keywords to assign one problem to multiple categories.

Instead of writing in an attribute, we might create a link from the problem report to specific note – perhaps the agent for that category. The agent now looks for notes that are linked to it:

Query: #linkedTo(Computer) | Text(internet) | ....

8. Links

Links are the distinctive feature of hypertext. Ever since the World Wide Web became ubiquitous, nearly everyone who has thought about them seems to have jumped to the conclusion that they intuitively understand links and their use.

Library scientists looked at links and saw a catalog. Engineers looked at links and saw a network. Scholars saw footnotes. Novelists saw a host of familiar literary and rhetorical devices – timeshift, recursus. Literary critics saw contemporary critical theory made manifest. Technical writers saw wire-bound manuals with effective cross-references. In the early years of hypertext research, everyone seemed to think that, while building a working system would be hard, they themselves knew *exactly* how to use links once we had them.

Everyone now knows that links are useful, because everyone uses them. A few people affect to express doubt on the subject, especially when applying for funds for research studies, but nobody genuinely doubts that people find hypertext useful for the same reason nobody doubts that people find cinema entertaining.

But there exists today no clear consensus of opinion, nor body of scientific observation, that demonstrates exactly how links are best used. There is not even a working consensus on how we might judge whether their use in a particular hypertext is effective or not. A common approach, to be sure, is to propose a particular task and then to demonstrate how the writer's own link technique is particularly suited to the job. Another writer proposes a different task. A third asks whether any of these tasks are realistic: after all, most of our reading (and, arguably, all of our most important reading) pursues tasks that we perceive dimly at best, or pursues no task at all.

A parallel development may be observed in discussion of the role of graphic design in hypertexts and Web sites. Though many designers currently share a rough consensus on what kind of

> typography and layout are readable and attractive,
> today's most visible and profitable Web sites ignore
> these principles. When the Web was still new, this
> defiance might have been blamed on ignorance or
> incompetence, but by now we must accept that
> eBay and Yahoo and CyWorld intend to look the
> way they do.

Over the years, I confess I have not often been reluctant to claim to know part of the answer to the link question. My answers have not (thus far) been generally adopted, nor have any of the alternatives met with widespread or sustained enthusiasm.

Tinderbox adopts a policy of least commitment: after more than fifteen years of discussion and experimentation, fundamental questions about the use and utility of links remain unresolved, and so Tinderbox is designed to support all sorts of linking styles and schemes. The underlying foundation for Tinderbox links is designed, moreover, so that Tinderbox's link mechanisms can grow as new ideas emerge and that may provide a foundation for further research.

Formalization and Link Types

Links in their various forms and in their different guises may well prove to be the great intellectual contribution of our generation. They lie at the core of the Web, the greatest library and most extensive computational medium the world has known. And hypertext links are distinct: they were anticipated in print by tables of contents, indexes, cross-references, footnotes, interlineations, the Talmud, the synoptic Gospels, by Egyptian wall painting, by many other antecedents, but clearly the hypertext link is a new phenomenon.

We know links are important, and we know they are useful. But what are links for?

One of the earliest and still most sophisticated approaches to the link was Randy Trigg's doctoral dissertation, which explored a hypertext system for reviewing scientific papers for publication [24]. Before a scientific paper is published in a journal, other scientists anonymously review it, seeking to identify any ambiguities or errors in the manuscript. This review is usually conducted with very great care and often involves subtle reasoning on issues both central and peripheral.

In 1986 – eight years before the Web – Trigg proposed and implemented a tool that is still more elaborate than today's state of the art, allowing referees to compose hypertextual evaluations of the work under discussion. Instead of composing conventional commentaries (which sometimes exceed the original paper in length), reviewers would write concise critiques of specific points and link them directly to the issues they address. Moreover, the links, in Trigg's view, would have *types*, drawn from a vocabulary of link types suited to reviewing scientific papers. In an appendix, Trigg usefully provides a detailed collection of relevant link types:

Normal Links	Specialize	Rewrite
Citation	Abstraction	Explanation
source	Example	Simplification
pioneer	Formalization	Complication
credit	Application	Update
leads	Argument	Correction
eponym	deduction	Continuation
Background	induction	
FutureWork	analogy	**Commentary Links**
Refutation	intuition	Comment
Support	solution	critical
Methodology	Summarization	supportive
Data	Detail	RelatedWork
Generalize	AlternateView	misrepresents

vacuum	arbitrary
ignores	unmotivated
isSupersededBy	Argumentation
isRefutedBy	invalid
isSupportedBy	insufficient
redundant	immaterial
ProblemPosing	misleading
trivial	alternative
unimportant	straw man
impossible	Data
ill-posed	inadequate
solved	dubious
ambitious	ignores
Thesis	irrelevant
trivial	inapplicable
unimportant	misinterpreted
irrelevant	Style
herring	boring
contradict	unimaginative
dubious	incoherent
counterexample	arrogant
inelegant	rambling
simplistic	awkward

After finishing his dissertation, Trigg went to Xerox PARC where he worked with Frank Halasz on NoteCards [8], a sophisticated early hypertext tool that, along with its successor Aquanet ("A hypertext tool to hold your knowledge in place" [15]), is one of the inspirations of Tinderbox.

Formality Considered Harmful: The Rejection of Link Types

Experience with typed links soon led researchers – most notably Trigg himself – to conclude that users did not want them and would not use them. If the vocabulary of link types is too small, then users cannot find a link type that expresses what they wish to say. As the vocabulary grows, however, choosing the correct link type becomes more and more difficult.

Reviewing a scientific paper is a short-lived and well-defined task. In such ephemeral work, it can seem wasteful to carefully select link types when the document itself may be read once or twice. Many submitted papers are clearly unacceptable, and some are quickly seen to be publishable if nobody finds a blunder; in either case, building complex argumentative webs of typed links that may only be read once seems tedious and wasteful. In cases like this, the added work required by link types seemed pointless.

More common notemaking tasks require more time and pursue larger goals, and in these efforts it was hoped that formal link types might yield greater rewards. The very scope of broader tasks, however, also created new headaches. Over time, users find their understanding increases. Link types that were chosen in the early days of the project eventually seem wrong, yet the effort of changing all these links may seem unjustified. Moreover, notes must often be made in haste; the user, struggling to capture inspiration and to jot down ideas swiftly, has no time for the subtle distinctions among related link types. In the event, people fell into the habit of choosing broad types simply to make the link quickly, and subsequently ignored the link type [16, 22].

At the same time, the complexity of writing (which the hypertext research community had initially underestimated) was gradually becoming clear. In particular, both critical theory [12] and careful examination of actual hypertexts [3] showed that it is often impossible to assign a single function or meaning to each unit of a text. The same link carries a different meaning in different contexts; worse, that meaning may well depend on what the reader has already seen, and what the reader already knows. A link might, in the first stages of a long project, represent an eager insight. Later, its more knowledgeable creator might look at the same link as a cautionary flag, an example of early naïveté. Still later, the same link might be seen as ironic commentary, or satire, or as a proposal for a daring and unexpected return to a long-abandoned position.

The Computational goto and the Navigation Problem

At the first Hypertext Conference, Andy van Dam – a hypertext pioneer who is best known as one of the fathers of computer graphics – delivered an influential keynote in which he compared the hypertext link with an obsolete programming language construct, the goto statement. Early programming languages depended on explicit goto instructions to move from one part of the program to another, encouraging programmers to improvise their own control flow. In the 1970s, though, a new wave of programmers discovered that a small vocabulary of control structures would, in fact, suffice for all situations; since these structures were sufficient, they argued, their use would encourage discipline and ease understanding and maintenance of programs. *Ad hoc* control structures prompted tangled "spaghetti" code, they argued, and the adoption of a small set of universal control structures (if/then branches, while loops, and recursive subroutines) would make programs easy to understand. Donald Knuth declared "GOTO Considered Harmful", Edsgar Dijkstra proposed *A Programming Discipline,* and spaghetti was banished from the computer programmer's table.

Van Dam, equating the link with the goto, was suggesting that hypertexts might more effectively be structured using a small set of richer relations. What these relations might be, however, proved difficult to envision, and few serious attempts were made to create a structural vocabulary or to demonstrate its sufficiency. Instead, van Dam's message was most clearly heard as a caution against hypertextual complexity and as a warning that, left to themselves, hypertext writers and their subject matter might well create tangles of meaning that would defy understanding.

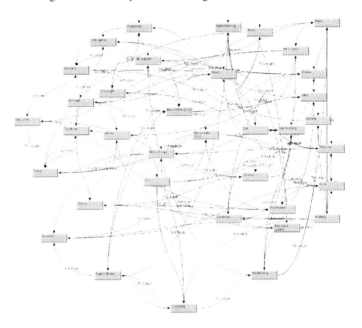

Figure 30. Hypertext map from Mary-Kim Arnold, "Lust", *Eastgate Quarterly Review of Hypertext* 1(2). The link network of a hypertext is often hard to understand at a glance.

Link Minimalism

Reacting to van Dam's warning, a number of workers adopted a vision of links that was essentially prescriptive: links should express the connection between modules of information, with each link performing a declared and defined role. Large documents, they suggested, could be mastered by hierarchical decomposition, using links to express structure. Links might also play a carefully limited role in drawing connections across the structure, providing glossaries or media services. The result was *link minimalism*, a hypertext movement which, ironically, sought to use links as little as possible. This impulse was expressed in *hypertext engineering* [7], Hypertext Design Methodology [6], and similar efforts to simplify and tame the potential complexity of the link network.

My own early hypertext work, in retrospect, fits into this line of development. The chief concern of "The Bookmark and The Compass" [2] was the fear that readers would find hypertexts disorienting and confusing; it proposed a host of tools – bookmarks, breadcrumbs, thumb tabs, margin notes – to remind readers where they were.

The lasting contribution of link minimalism, in the end, was its attempt to draw a distinction between *structural* links, which were intended to express the articulation of the hypertext into sections and subsections, and "applicative" links which were intended to express connections relating to the subject matter or "application" of the document. In small documents and in new projects, structural links provided a powerful framework for planning hypertexts and for coordinating teams of writers, and this function finds its echo in the Tinderbox outline view. The same duality is reflected in contemporary Web design, which frequently separates structural links in navigation bars while placing applicative links within the text.

The Confrontation with Critical Theory

The program of the link minimalists was doomed from the outset because the minimalists, fearing to abandon the comforting affordances of the codex, failed to perceive that 20th-century criticism had already abandoned the position they sought to defend. For the minimalists, in the end, wanted to rely on structural links to capture the single essential structure of the hypertext; literary theory, inconveniently for the minimalists, had by this time definitively abandoned the belief that writing possesses a single structure.

The initial encounter between hypertext research and critical theory took place near the end of the Second Hypertext Conference, when Stuart Moulthrop read a dense paper on "Hypertext and The Hyperreal" [19] to a Hilton ballroom that overflowed with puzzled computer scientists. Moulthrop tried to reconcile Baudrillard's attack on simulated experience and the Disneyfication of American culture with hypertext's mediation of print, but few in the audience had heard of Baudrillard. In the aftermath it was clear that Moulthrop lost the audience – one distinguished scientist asked whether the talk had been a satire. But Moulthrop, together with George P. Landow and Frank Halasz, did manage to direct attention to a growing body of experimental hypertext fiction and theory, especially Michael Joyce's hypertext *afternoon, a story* [9] and its discussion in Jay David Bolter's monograph, *Writing Space* [4]. Hypertext engineers, trained in the sciences, had assumed that writing was (or should be) a simple matter of design and instantiation. We were (for, at this point, I was numbered among them) believers in New Criticism at a time when New Critics were already extinct.

If the reception of Moulthrop's paper showed how large the chasm was, his hypertext novel *Victory Garden* [20] made a crucial contribution to bridging it. Joyce's *afternoon,* though widely admired, was not widely understood. Moulthrop's episodic novel about the first Gulf War and the ongoing controversy of the canon then embroiling world campuses was a convincing demonstration of hypertext's power – and of its complexity. Moulthrop's links are filled with puns, tricks, feints, and deceptions. No one can believe these links can be clearly labeled, or that they epitomize "free and knowing navigation" [21], and yet these links are also clearly planned with care and intelligence. For a time, link minimalists tried to argue informally that such effects would prove useful only in the arts, but David Kolb, a philosopher, published *Socrates in the Labyrinth* [10] to preempt this line of argument by showing that the philosophical underpinnings of argumentation were at least as complex as the artistic effects the minimalists sought to dismiss.

In the end, it became clear that links could carry multiple meanings, and that the meaning of a link often depends on its context, on what the reader has already seen, and on information the reader brings to the reading.

Navigation

Trigg's link types declare what a link *is*. A second line of development asks links to carry an operational, rather than a formal, meaning. Links, in this view, say nothing about what their endpoints are or what their relationship may be; they offer an opportunity to go from one place to another.

This functional view of links as a tool for getting around was reinforced by an accidental Web idiom. Web URLs describe how to locate a particular page on a Web server; since almost all early Web servers stored data in a hierarchical file system, URLs acquired a strong topical flavor.

> http://...server.../press/ProductAnnouncement.html
> http://...server.../products/consumer/D703.html
> http://...server.../blog/2003/03/22.html

Because Web pages were stored in a file system and because URLs themselves reflected this hierarchy, it seemed natural to assume that the hierarchy would reflect the structure of the site and that the principal role of links would be to help visitors move from the "home" page to the section of the site in which they were chiefly interested. Links, in this view, compete with search as a tool for getting to the right place.

If links were poorly chosen – if the site structure wasn't intuitive or clearly expressed – designers feared that users would become disoriented, lost in a tangle of links or frustrated at their inability to locate desired information. In practice, though, naïve Web readers found the very notion of disorientation to be a puzzling academic notion. "I know where I am," users would tell investigators over and over again, "I'm on this page at **something.com.** It's not where I want to be, I suppose, but I'm not disoriented."

Nothing requires Web sites to be stored as static files, just as nothing requires the file storage to reflect the topical organization of the site. Database-backed sites – sites where the URL reflected the needs of a database query tool rather than a

hierarchical file system – began to erode the
presumption that the physical organization of files
would reflect the way those files would be used.
Web 2.0 sites return to meaningful URLs, but the
URLs no longer describe actual files; instead, the
URL is simply a convenient format for passing
information to a Web service.

More recently, frustrated attempts to build large sites and indexes based on a grand taxonomy – a single, consensual, topical organization – led to enthusiasm for informal folksonomies and *ad hoc* tag schemes. But tag clouds and folksonomies necessarily abandon the hope of an ideal or optimal navigation scheme in which everything finds its proper place. Informal organization demands informal (and multiple) navigation.

Indeed, while minimalists tried to eliminate as many confusing links as they could and navigationalists strove to make links universally clear and intuitive, some hypertext writers were deliberately seeking to disorient readers, and found the work surprisingly difficult.

Trying To Get Lost

Why would a writer *want* readers to be disoriented?

First, a common initial task of an instructor is to break up false confidence and mistaken preconceptions. Students arrive in the university lecture hall (and, indeed, in middle school classrooms) filled with youthful confidence in the depth of their understanding and the excellence of their judgment. In order to get anywhere, an instructor may need to show them what they don't know – to confuse them.

Second, a number of hypertext fiction writers felt an urgent need, at some points, to elaborate and obscure the hypertext structure, preventing readers from forming a simple mental picture of the work. Many of these writers sought to reject or transcend familiar narrative conventions, especially the familiar safety of television melodrama. Others were eager to lead readers by unexpected paths to return to *lexia* they had read before, but which would take on new meaning when revisited.

What was striking here was not that these writers wanted to disorient readers, but rather how hard they had to work to do it. In *afternoon*, Michael Joyce builds a maze of tiny lexia. Elsewhere in the same work, he creates shadow pages that closely resemble the text of places the reader has already seen, but which have different links. Carolyn Guyer's *Quibbling* presents an image of myriad colored kites in the sunlight – with each kite linked to a different hypertext path. Mary-Kim Arnold's *Lust* begins with a lyric poem, every word of which leads to a different path through the hypertext.

Keeping Things Connected

Links have proven to be much more complex and much less tractable than we once expected. The difficulties surrounding links even led some to reject them entirely. Spatial hypertext (Chapter 16) replaces links with *ad hoc* spatial arrangements. Link minimalism seeks to avoid and simplify links. Current Web practice sometimes urges writers to avoid links entirely, fearing that links could interrupt attention or encourage the reader to visit some other site.

Can we dispense with links entirely? By focusing too closely on what links cannot do, we may overlook tasks at which links excel.

Retaining connection in the face of revision. When taking notes, we often find that two pieces of information are intrinsically connected, and that the connection should almost certainly be retained across any future revision. Often, for example, we may copy down a memorable quotation and link it to its source. That connection needs to remain solid, whatever cutting and pasting, reconceptualizing and reorganization our notes undergo. We might have originally envisioned the quotation in chapter six, move it months later to chapter 13, and then decide that part of it belongs instead in chapter 9. Wherever it goes, we want to remember its source.

Similarly, if we are investigating a crime or choosing a vendor, we will gather opinions and facts from many sources. The data are our first concern, but we want to record their sources as well, because subsequent analysis may reveal that some information was tainted by bias or self-interest, or that certain informants were especially reliable.

Representing One-To-One Relationships. Some relationships inherently connect exactly two notes. Tinderbox's notion of *prototype,* for example, asserts that an instance has one specific prototype – every property of the note that isn't otherwise specified is referred to the prototype. This connection can be represented very naturally by a link.

Discovery and The Scent Of Information. By presenting a pathway from one note to another, links help us move rationally and intentionally through the space of notes and ideas. An effective, intelligent link network helps facilitate our use of notes by guiding us through them.

When we are looking for a half-remembered idea or a misplaced observation, links complement search. Search works well when we are seeking a specific text pattern, such as a name or a date. Search is less reliable, though, when we can describe what sort of note we're seeking, but don't remember precisely what words it might contain. In this case, links can often guide us closer and closer to the note in which we are interested.

Folding Space. In a spatial hypertext, proximity takes on special, semantic meaning. Adjacent notes, or notes that lie on the same adornment or cluster together, are connected. Distant notes are separated. At times, however, we may need to "fold" space, to assert a connection between notes that cannot be clustered together. Here, the link might not represent a one-to-one relationship; we might link a *representative* note in one cluster to some *representative* note in another cluster to remind us that these widely separated clusters are, in fact, related.

For example, one cluster of notes might represent product definition and development tasks that are currently assigned to a group of designers. A second cluster of notes represents ongoing press and investor relations initiatives assigned to a Marketing Communications department. For most purposes, these activities are disparate – they are performed within different organizations by people who report to different managers. Still, some design initiatives will require market communications; once the product features are chosen, we'll need a product announcement. Similarly, some PR activities require design support: before we can approve final advertising designs, the design group will need to deliver a product prototype for photography. Links can represent typical or sensitive connections between these otherwise separate activities.

The Space Between: Examining Relationships

The process of linking notes together forces us to reflect on their relationship and can lead us to discover ideas and connections that were not initially evident. Building these connections can present exciting pedagogical opportunities. George Landow's classes in Victorian Literature have, for example, created over the years a vast web of short essays and original sources. Most of this Web originated in student assignments and class readings; in most institutions, this work would have been graded and discarded. Instead, *The Victorian Web* has generated two published hypertexts and, in its Web version, receives millions of hits each month[13].

A very interesting, albeit anecdotal, series of observations on the impact of linking was reported by Pam Taylor, a professor of Art Education whose doctoral research involved a two-year project in which high school students created hypertextual art portfolios in Storyspace [23]. Each new work had to be added to the portfolio and linked to the student's previous work – not least because these links allowed the teacher to find and evaluate the new assignments!

Over time, though, students found that the effort to draw connections among their work led them to think again about their earlier efforts and, more significantly, to discover themes and changes in their art. One student, whom Taylor calls "Lindsay", had tended to be quiet and withdrawn, reluctant to participate in the classroom.

> *Lindsay was very uncomfortable with the kinds of discussions that went on in her art class. She was quiet and only answered or offered discussion when she was called upon directly. Even then, she would simply regurgitate what the teacher had said previously, or ask, "What do you want me to say?"*

Over the course of the two-year class, however, Lindsay's efforts to find connections in her work, and connections to other art she enjoyed and admired, led her to conclude that her personal relationships were unsatisfactory and, indeed, abusive. In the process of drawing connections, Lindsay discovered for herself (and also found ways to discuss with her instructor) a theme in her art practice of which she had not been aware. Taylor reports that

> *Lindsay's experiences working in her computer web appeared to provide her a comfortable space to begin thinking and challenging the artwork that she studied and her ideas about herself....*

> *It is impossible to overlook the fact that Lindsay viewed her study and life differently after her hypertextual experience. She no longer simply absorbed whatever information was delivered by her teachers, textbooks, or friends. Through the self-directed exploration made possible by her work in her computer web, Lindsay began to assert her voice as a student, an artist, and a young woman. She carried this newfound voice from the computer, into the art class and her life.*

Finally, it is vital to consider the meaning of the link, the manner in which readers extract information from the link and its trajectory. When we follow a navigation link from *here* to *there*, we naturally inquire why the link was made as it was. What did the link's label suggest we would find at its destination? How does this explanation refract our encounter with the destination text? The link situates the meaning of its source and destination while carrying its own *interstitial* meaning in the chasm between one note and another. The connection between links and the cinematic cut (and Eisenstein's theory of montage) is intimate and requires careful thought [17, 18].

Design Note: Internal and External Links

Even the most familiar form of link – the simple connection from one text selection to another – created a protracted implementation dispute that concealed what is, in fact, a deeper disagreement about the expected behavior of links. This dispute arose from what seemed

at first a simple programming question: where will the hypertext
system store the link's description?

Some hypertext systems represent links by embedding them in the
text. The Web, for example, indicates a link anchor by adding some
special text inside the page:

<a href="http://www.eastgate.com"> Eastgate </a>

This is an *internal* link [5], and it has one cardinal advantage: if we
need to edit the text inside the link, we can insert or delete characters
as we wish without invalidating the link.

This is not the only possible way to represent links; we might, for
example, have a table outside the text which lists the start and end of
each link:

Start: 1 End: 8 href: http://www.eastgate.com

This table is separate from the text; it might be stored elsewhere in
the same file, or it might be stored in a separate file entirely. This is
an *external link*, and it, too, has a cardinal advantage: if the links are
stored separately, we can easily add additional links – or even replace
one network of links with a completely new network – whenever we
wish without changing the text itself. (If we ever do change the text,
of course, we need to check all the links that refer to it and update
their offsets.)

The history of hypertext has been marked by many implementation
controversies, but this particular conflict masks a fundamental
dispute over the nature and malleability of texts[5]. Internal links
encourage malleable texts – editing is no more difficult than
conventional text editing – but internal links imply that the owner of
the text controls all outbound links. If you want to let readers
annotate, you either have to give them indiscriminate permission to
edit the page [14] or you need to support external links. If you want
to support external links, you must either avoid editing the page or
you need an elaborate notification service to update all the link tables
whenever the page changes.

External links favor open systems where different users may employ different tools to read and write link networks. Ownership of linking is separated from ownership of the underlying document. While some attention has been paid to providing operating system support for updating external links, this is clearly a difficult problem. External link advocates are often document-centric, treating the nodes as fixed and unchanging atoms. (Indeed, it is an explicit requirement of Nelson's Xanadu that texts never change; new versions may be created but a text, once published, remains forever unaltered.)

Tinderbox Links

Tinderbox straddles the fence. Following Storyspace, Tinderbox actually implements text and Web links as *external* but makes them appear to be *internal*. The external links are stored in the same file as the rest of the document, but links are separated from the text and not embedded in it. Since Tinderbox handles text editing internally, it can easily update its links as needed.

Structural links, on the other hand, are handled separately in Tinderbox. Since text editing does not modify the document hierarchy, no notification mechanism is needed.

9. Sharing Lists and Outlines

Sharing Lists

Often, the things we want to share on personal information pages (Chapter 10) are lists:

> Bibliographies
>
> Navigational lists and sidebars
>
> Blogrolls and reading lists
>
> ToDo lists, task lists, milestones and deliverables
>
> Lists of books we have recently read, or films we
> have seen
>
> Photographic albums and art galleries

Within Tinderbox, lists may be represented as containers, agents, or simply as text lists written inside notes.

In HTML, lists are enclosed in list tags such as <ul>...</ul> (unordered lists) or <ol>...</ol> (ordered lists), while individual items are enclosed in list-item tags, <li>...</li>.

How can we most conveniently move from Tinderbox to HTML list markup?

Quick Lists

Where lists are embedded in text, Tinderbox lets us quickly signal
that a word or phrase is part of a list and not a conventional
paragraph. For an unordered list, we place an asterisk at the start of
each item

> *ducks
> ** grebes
> ** dabbling ducks
> ** diving ducks
> *hawks
> *owls
> *passerines

As illustrated here, nested lists are indicated by multiple asterisks.
Ordered lists are indicated in the same manner, but use the
octothorpe '#'

> #Augustus
> #Tiberius
> #Claudius
> #Caligula
> #Nero

When you export a quick list to HTML, Tinderbox removes the
markers "*" and "#" and inserts the appropriate HTML list markup.
The list markup, moreover, can be customized as needed by changing
the value of Tinderbox attributes. **HTMLListStart** and **HTMLListEnd**
are the tags that represent the start and end of unordered lists,
HTMLOrderedListStart/End mark the start and end of ordered lists,
and **HTMLListItemStart/End** mark the start and end of lists items.
You can easily change these attributes for individual notes with a
QuickStamp or in the note's Get Info window. Changing the default
value of the attributes can change the markup throughout the
document.

Tip: changing QuickList markup is most often used
to apply a special CSS style to a specific list. For

example, HTMLListStart might take the value <ul
class="navigation"> in headers and footers.

Containers and Agents: The List Wrapper Idiom

When quick lists grow long or complex, we may long for Tinderbox's powerful list-management tools. Fortunately, it is easy to use the Explode command to split a quick list into a group of individual notes, and equally easy to reassemble those notes into a shared HTML list.

Instead of listing items within a note's text, we might list them as child notes inside the note, which now serves as a container. In the text or the template of the container, we use ^justChildren to export a list item for each note in the container:

Figure 31. A list of project milestones might be exported as a checklist for the wall, a bullet list for a management report, and a navigational sidebar for the volunteer Web site.

Milestones for the current development campaign include:
<ul> ^justChildren(myListItemTemplate) </ul>

^justChildren will export each note in the container in turn, applying to each of these notes the export template "myListItemTemplate". This template tells Tinderbox how to handle each item within the list, and may be very simple:

<li> ^title^ </li>

Occasionally, we might want to include additional information in the template:

<li> ^title^ ^get(Deadline,"d M y") </li>

If it is inconvenient to include the list items as children of the note, we may instead gather the list items in a separate container. Our text now uses ^include rather than ^justChildren:

Milestones for the current development campaign include:
^include(MilestoneList, myLstTemplate)

The container MilestoneList has its own template

<ul> ^justChildren(myListItemTemplate) </ul>

Thus, the list is constructed by two templates. The first, **myListTemplate**, formats the start and end of the list and then invokes the second, **myListItemTemplate**, for each member of the list. We call the outer template the "list wrapper"; this two-template idiom is very common, flexible, and powerful.

Sharing Outlines

The most powerful way to share Tinderbox outlines, of course, is to share them as Tinderbox files. Tinderbox document files are easy to email and compact enough to be easily uploaded and downloaded. Colleagues and collaborators can use Tinderbox to review your outlines, and then they can add their own comments (perhaps using the Note tool). They can easily copy notes or entire sections into their personal Tinderbox documents.

> **Tip:** Even if your colleagues don't have a copy of Tinderbox, they can use the free Tinderbox demonstration to explore your Tinderbox documents. If you need to equip a work group or team with Tinderbox, Eastgate offers 10-user, 50-user, and 100-user licenses.

At times, though, you'll want to share outlines on the Web as summaries or extracts of larger documents. Some common scenarios include:

- planning documents and preliminary drafts for discussion
- summaries of larger documents, programs, or enterprises
- organizational charts
- navigational tools or sidebars for Web sites

Tinderbox provides a variety of flexible and convenient ways to share outlines on the Web.

Outlines Styles

HTML represents outlines as lists. Ordered lists – lists whose items are to be numbered in sequence – are introduced with the <ol> tag. Unordered lists – lists where items are marked with symbols like bullets (•) or not marked at all – are introduced with the <ul> tag. Each item in a list is enclosed by a list item tag, <li>

```
<ul>
        <li> Item 1</li>
        <li> Item 2</li>
</ul>
```
In a browser, this list will appear something like this:

• Item 1

• Item 2

Lists can contain lists, too, and this is the key to presenting outlines in HTML. For example:

```
<ol>
        <li> Zeus </li>
        <ol type="a">
                <li>Athena </li>
                <li> Apollo </li>
        </ol>
```

```
<li> Hera </li>
<li> Aphrodite </li>
<li> Hermes </li>
</ol>
```
will be formatted like this:

1. Zeus
   a. Athena
   b. Apollo
2. Hera
3. Aphrodite
4. Hermes

The *type* of the list gives the browser a clue about how you would prefer the list to appear. For ordered lists, type="a" suggests that letters be used instead of numbers, while type="I" suggests Roman numerals. For unordered lists, type="disc" marks each item with an "o" instead of a bullet.

For advanced users, stylesheets can control how lists appear on the page. For example, instead of displaying each list element on its own line, we may run them together horizontally:

About Us News Order Contact

This sort of list is common for Web navigation. The HTML list remains very simple.

```
<ul class="navigation>
<li> About Us </li>
<li> News </li>
<li> Order </li>
<li> Contact </li>
</ul>
```

All the details for the presentation are included in the stylesheet:

```
ul li {
    font-size: small;
    display: inline;
    padding-right: 20px;
}
```

We can easily change the appearance of the list. In the example above, each item is separated with 20 pixels of empty space, Instead, we might create a set of "tabs" from the same markup, simply by changing the stylesheet:

```
ul {
    border-bottom: black;
    border-width: 0 0 1px 0;
    border-style: none none solid none;
    padding-bottom: 4px;
    font-family: sans-serif;
}
```

```
ul li {
    font-size: small;
    display: inline;
    color: black;
    background-color: #ccc;
    border-width: 1px;
    border-style: solid;
    border-color: #000;
    margin-left: 0px;
    padding: 4px 10px 4px 10px;
    margin-right: 5px;
}
```

Stylesheets are especially handy for sharing Tinderbox lists and outlines, because they help to separate the simple concept of a list, with its simple markup, from the sometimes demanding and complicated requirements of typesetting and graphic design. All

Tinderbox needs to worry about is exporting the list; stylesheets handle the formatting.

Snapshots from Tinderbox

Organizing and moving items in lists are particular strengths of Tinderbox's chart and outline views. One fast and simple way to share the current structure of a complex or fast-changing section of a Tinderbox document is, simply, to capture a screen shot or image of a view.

Choose **Copy View Picture** from the edit menu to place an image from the current view on the clipboard, ready to paste into your word processor or image editor.

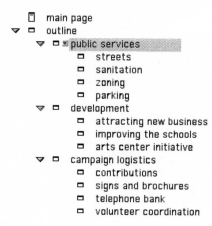

Figure 32. The image of an outline, copied from a Tinderbox view

Sharing pictures lets you capture the colors, fonts, magnification, and outline state of your Tinderbox document, so your audience can see exactly what you want to show them. By providing an image, you can avoid worrying about browser incompatibilities and formatting problems. But images are, in some ways, less useful to your audience. Since you're only providing a picture, your readers can't copy crucial items to paste into their own work. Instead, they'll have to retype anything they want to use – even if they only want to send you a comment or correction.

Exporting an Outline

Fortunately, you can also use Tinderbox export templates to build an outline of the hierarchical structure of any section of your Tinderbox document. Let's revisit the document in Figure 32, with an eye to putting an outline of the section inside the container named "Outline" somewhere on the main page.

First, let's write a simple template, called *SimpleOutline*

```
<li>^title^</li>

^if(^get(ChildCount))
    <ol>
^justChildren(SimpleOutline)
    </ol>
^endif
```

This template exports a note's name, marked up as a list item. Then, if the note happens to contain children, it builds a nested list of those children.

In the main note, include the outline like this:

```
<ol> ^include(outline,SimpleOutline)^ </ol>
```

If we preview "Main Page" in our browser, we'll see something like this:

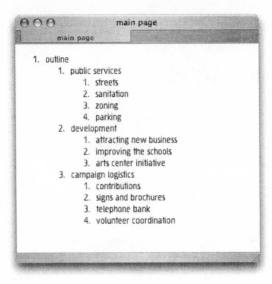

Figure 33. A preview of our outline, exported with the SimpleOutline template

Notice how straightforward this is; a single template handles everything. The outline can extend to whatever depth we like; whenever a note discovers that it contains other notes, it builds its own subsection of the outline.

VARIATIONS

The outline container's title is shown at the top of the outline. Perhaps you'd prefer to format it as a heading? Just define a new template, *SimpleOutlineContainer*.

```
<h1>^title^</h1>

^if(^get(ChildCount))
        <ol> ^justChildren(SimpleOutline)
        </ol>
^endif
```

We no longer need the list markup in the text of "Main Page":

```
^include(outline,SimpleOutlineContainer)^
```

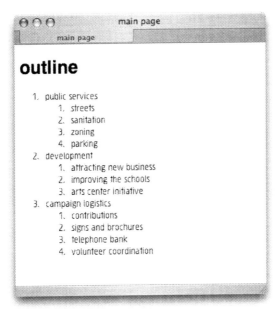

Figure 34. We export using SimpleOutlineContainer for the top level of the outline. It generates a heading, and then exports the outline as before.

Of course, we can omit the heading entirely by making the SimpleOutlineContainer template even simpler:

```
^if(^get(ChildCount))
        <ol> ^justChildren(SimpleOutline)
        </ol>
^endif
```

Now, the container exports only its children – not itself.

If we like, we can include more information in the outline. For example, we might modify the SimpleOutline template to tell us how much text is contained in each item:

<li> ^title^ (^get(Wordcount^ words) </li>

Or, we might want to keep track of the date when each item was last revised:

<li> ^title^: ^get(Modified,"L") </li>

> 1. public services: Tuesday, March 9, 2004
>   1. streets: Friday, April 16, 2004

Figure 35. Each item is now annotated with the date when it was last revised, displayed in the user's preferred date format.

More complex logic is easy to add as well.

- For a "business dashboard", we might apply styles to critical items – those that have changed recently and those that have gone far too long without revision – and use a stylesheet to display those items in a distinctive color or typeface.
- To reduce information overload, we might add additional data only when it is especially useful. For example, we might display the revision date only for items changed in the last week:

^if(^^days(^Modified,7)) New! ^get(Modified,"L")
^endif

Templates as Subroutines

In a sense, templates can act as procedures or subroutines. The *SimpleOutlineContainer* "calls" *SimpleOutline*, which recursively calls itself to format the outline.

We can use this way of thinking to simplify tasks that seem complex. For example, suppose we'd like to mix alphabetic and numerical labels. The outside level of the outline will be labeled with letters, the next level with numbers. We can do this easily by defining two templates. *outline_numeric* is just like *SimpleOutline*, but it builds nested lists with alphabetic labels.

```
<li>^title^ </li>
^if(^get(ChildCount))
        <ol type="a"> ^justChildren(outline_alpha)
        </ol>
^endif
```

The second template, *outline_alpha,* formats lists inside itself numerically.

```
<li>^title^</li>

^if(^get(ChildCount))
        <ol type="1"> ^justChildren(outline_numeric)
        </ol>

^endif
```

Now, if the *OutlineContainer* formats its children with *Outline_Numeric,* its grandchildren will be formatted with *outline_alpha.* Numeric calls Alpha, and Alpha calls Numeric.

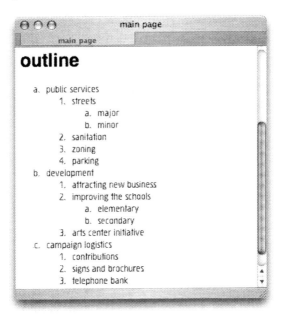

Figure 36. Alphabetic and numeric labels alternate with each generation.

This approach is both flexible and robust. Adding or moving items is easy, and the numbering will be automatically updated the next time you export. Adding new outline levels, as before, requires no special work; the templates will choose the appropriate list style as needed. Nothing depends on the position of the section of interest within the Tinderbox document as a whole; so we're free to move it whenever we like.

10. Sharing Notes: Personal Information Pages

Personal Information Pages

Not everyone needs a weblog or an elaborate commerce site, but almost everyone needs some web presence. We have come to expect that nearly any legitimate business will have a telephone listing, and more recently that it will have at least a simple Web presence. Increasingly, we expect that people we meet will also have a Web contact point, a place where we can readily find public information.

Suppose your second cousin Bess wants to invite you to her daughter's wedding: she needs a way to find you. Suppose you meet someone at a party, and six months later they have a question for you – if only they knew how to get in touch. A former colleague or an ex-student wants to inquire about some work you did together years ago; how do they locate you? The Personal Information Page is a Web site for people who don't want a Web site, a home page for people who don't live on the Web.

> Tip: Even if you maintain an elaborate Web presence or weblog, you need a personal information page. A remarkable number of weblog writers, for example, forget to say who they are. Even for anonymous writing, the reader wants and deserves to know something about the writer. Are these the opinions of a child or an adult? Of an interested amateur or an expert authority? Of an interested participant or a sympathetic observer?

A personal information page should be complete, current and accurate. It should contain all the information you desire to be part of your public identity. Different people will want to disclose different things, of course. A writer should probably list their work, since the reader might well know them only through their books and articles. Some neighborhood activists might mention their children, since the neighbors might well know Jon and Betsy much better than their parents. I list my email address and office phone so that readers and customers can reach me; a movie actor might instead provide contact information for their agent. Whatever we decide to include, the information is likely to be varied, and it's likely to change. We need to organize all this information, we want to make it easy to maintain, and we'd like to separate the information from the details of its appearance.

> Tip: We might want to change the appearance of our Web page or our résumé from time to time. If the layout and content are mixed together, revisions tend to be difficult and distracting. By separating form and content, you can make it easier to keep information current while also making it easier to improve its appearance.

Tinderbox can work nicely in this role. We can use agents to extract key elements from a larger, private ToDo list. Or, we can simply drag things into the Pip as we need them. Tinderbox takes care of organizing and formatting. Most importantly, it's easy to add things – and Tinderbox can automatically sort the lists that ought to be sorted and hide the details that ought to be hidden.

The Simplicity of the Web

The Web is many things – an encyclopedia, a place to shop, a publication and broadcast medium. Here, though, we are concerned with the Web at its simplest and most fundamental level – as an efficient, inexpensive, and ubiquitous way of sharing information.

The underlying idea of the Web is very simple – so simple, beneath the elegant encrustations of elaborate scripting languages and stylesheets and graphic designs, that it is easily overlooked. That core idea is the **URL** – an address at which a hunk of information can be found. You place the information in a file on your Web server, and anyone can request the information by asking the server for whatever happens to reside at that address.

The simplicity of the Web has profound consequences:

- Because all Web requests are essentially identical, the server doesn't need to work very hard or need very much time to respond. The Web server can be small and simple.
- Because Web servers can be small and simple, they are cheap and ubiquitous.
- Because storing small files (and notes, of course, are usually small) is so inexpensive (see "Storage is Free", chapter 1), the cost of sharing your notes through the Web is negligible.

As You Like It

The places at which we share our notes may be loosely described as personal information pages or personal Web sites. Of course, the same mechanism can be used by entities that are not individual people. Political campaigns share notes. So do businesses, and project teams within a larger enterprise. Students and study groups share notes. And, since almost any medium will be used to create and present art, fictional characters may have personal Web sites, too.

Personal Web sites are *personal.* People often want their sites to express their individuality. When the site is generated with the aid of a power tool such as Tinderbox, it's important that the constraints imposed by the tool should not contradict the message or obstruct the purpose of the site.

Business Web sites are even more *personal* than individual sites. Corporations need to present a single face and a single message, to speak with one voice; when lots of employees say different things in different ways, nobody outside the company knows what's right and what's reliable. This is a question of branding and control, of course, but consistency and coherence run to the essence of corporate life: if the corporation is to be a single entity and not merely a big group of individual employees, more or less allied, then the business needs a single voice.

Pundits sometimes make fun of the teenage blogger who simply *must* have her Web page appear with purple type and curlicues, but no teenager is more precise or idiosyncratic in demanding visual style than a modern corporation. From Disney's signature to DuPont's red oval, from Google's playful simplicity to Berkshire Hathaway's staid plain text, the look and the interface have to adhere to detailed and inflexible standards.

As a *personal* content management assistant, Tinderbox needs to be equally comfortable with the demands of personal expression and corporate coherence. Indeed, these demands often coincide. Once you've gathered and analyzed your notes, when the time comes to share them, it's essential that Tinderbox helps you present them exactly the way you want.

> One key to making sure your Web work looks
> exactly the way you want is to master Cascading
> Style Sheets (CSS), a Web standard that helps you
> specify separately what the page or site will say,
> and how it should look. CSS was slow to be
> adopted because older browsers did not
> understand it or, worse, misunderstood it. By 2003,
> however, it was clear that these older browsers
> were becoming sufficiently rare that they were no
> longer of much concern.

Simple Templates

A *template* describes a way we'd like to export some information from Tinderbox notes for sharing. We often assume that sharing will be through the World Wide Web, because Web sites are so common, but the same mechanism that we use to export HTML will also work nicely with many other kinds of files.

- HTML files for sharing information with other people
- XML files for sharing information with other computers
- RSS files for syndicating updates to news sites and weblogs

The underlying export mechanism is simple and elegant. When you Export a document, Tinderbox examines each note in the file. Some notes might be marked "Don't Export"; we skip these. Sometimes, entire sections may be marked "Don't Export"; we skip these, too. For each note that *is* exported, Tinderbox follows a simple procedure.

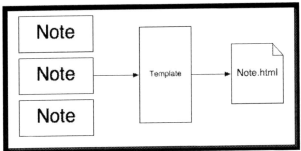

Figure 37. Each note that is to be exported is first poured into a template. The template determines exactly what parts of the note are exported and how these parts are presented.

First, we read the Export Template for the note. This is a file, much like the exported file we want to create, but it contains *placeholders* where Tinderbox is to insert information from the note we're exporting. For example, the template:

    Title: ^title^

will create a file with a single line that contains the title of the note. If we use this template to export a note named "The Tinderbox Way", the exported file will read

    Title: The Tinderbox Way

Similarly, if we change the template to

    ^Get(Modified,"l") ***** ^title

the file will read something like

    5 Jan 2011 ***** The Tinderbox Way

The template mechanism is extremely simple: Tinderbox simply makes a new file for each exported note and copies the template into it, replacing each placeholder with information taken from the note.

Where is the Template?

When exporting each note, Tinderbox needs to select the appropriate export template. The export template – like nearly everything in Tinderbox – is stored in an attribute. Here, the attribute is HTMLExportTemplate; if no export template is specified, the default value for HTMLExportTemplate is set in the HTML Export pane of the Preferences dialog.

> Tip: Always set the default export template preference. It's usually best to choose a simple template for the default, since simple templates are easier to debug.

All HTML export templates for a document must be stored in a single folder.

> Tip: When starting to work on a new Tinderbox document that I know will need export templates, I usually make two folders right away – one to hold the templates and the other to hold the exported files.

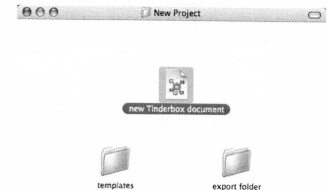

Understanding, not Magic

Working with templates, you can sometimes get by – for a while – without knowing much about what you're exporting. In the long run, though, you want to understand what you want to export, and why.

If you understand the files you're trying to build, you can compare what you have and what you want; that comparison will almost always reveal exactly how you want to change the template.

> **Tip:** Templates are simple – so simple, in fact, that it's easy to get carried away and create dozens of specialized templates, each interacting with others. If your templates do become confusing, don't panic. Take things step by step, starting from the simplest templates, and consult HTMLView frequently. HTMLView shows you exactly what Tinderbox is doing, so you can easily explore even the most complex template systems.

If, on the other hand, you're trying to build Web pages without knowing HTML, then either things work or they don't. If they don't work, you don't really have a plan or a direction. You can tinker – add this, delete that – and see if it helps. This is believing in magic.

Fortunately, learning about HTML (or XML, if that's what you need to export) is simple. You can find excellent introductions on the Web, and a host of guides at your local library or bookstore. Spending two or three hours with a good book (or a skilled friend) can give you the tools for building a working mastery. The magic may be gone, but so, too, will the mysterious incantations.

When templates don't work exactly as you expect them to, open an HTMLView window or examine the exported file in your favorite editor, or use your browser's View Source to look at the data. Figure out what's wrong; know that, and you'll know how to fix the templates.

Boilerplate: In The Template, or ^include?

Many Web sites include some fixed text or images on every page. For example, we might want to place some contact information at the bottom of every page:

Headquarters | London | Paris | New York | email us

If you created each page by hand, you'd place this at the end of every page. But, when you open a new branch in Rome, you'd need to edit every page to insert the extra link. That's time-consuming and error-prone.

One of the advantages of using a personal *content management* assistant for sharing information is that you can keep information like this in one place, and let the assistant automatically place it on every page. Using a mechanism to carry out mechanical changes like this is a good allocation of resources. You'll spend less time on corrections, and your results will contain fewer mistakes and inconsistencies.

For example, we could place the repeated information in the export template.

```
....
^text^
<div class="footer">
        <a href="HQ.html> Headquarters </a> |
        <a href="London.html> London </a> |
        <a href="Paris.html> Paris </a> |
        <a href="NY.html> New York </a> |
        <a href="contact.html> email us </a>
</div>
</body><html>
```

Every page that uses this template will conclude with the same footer. If we want to change the footer, we can simply change the template; we change the information once and the change appears on each individual page.

Alternatively, we could create a note, called **Footer**, that will hold the text and links for the footer. Our export template is now even simpler:

```
^text^
^include(footer)
</body><html>
```

For the footer note, we simply type the text and links in the text window. Its export template is a very simple file we'll call JustText; which simply exports the note's text:

```
^text
```

We can keep the Footer note simple by setting a few attributes in HTMLView.

HTMLFirstParagraphStart: <div class="footer">

HTMLFirstParagraphEnd: </div>

ExportTemplate: JustText

The resulting export is now identical to the first example.

Which solution is better? Putting the boilerplate in the template is straightforward, fast, and makes it harder to change the boilerplate accidentally. Using **^include** simplifies the template (though it adds a second, very simple, template) and makes it easier to modify the boilerplate quickly if you need to make frequent changes.

Assembling One Page From Many Notes

Often, Web designers and Information Architects think of a single Web page as a composite – a mixture of different kinds of information.

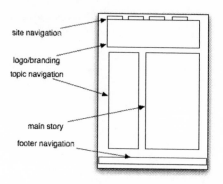

site navigation

logo/branding
topic navigation

main story
footer navigation

Figure 38. A conceptual or wireframe diagram that describes a family of
related Web pages within a site.

This sort of abstraction lets us design a family of related pages – each
of which will have a unique role and contain different information –
so that they retain a consistent appearance and so that they work
together and support each other. Different kinds of navigation, for
example, appear in consistent places on each page, encouraging pages
to take advantage of each other rather than repeating the same
information in many places. The same principle lets us design for
change, since the general scheme of the wireframe lets us plan how
we'll present pages we have not yet created, and how they'll be linked
to related pages so that readers will discover them.

Several markup elements help you pull information from different
notes into a single Web page:

^include(note[,template])	includes information from another note, formatted using the specified template
^justChildren([template])	includes information from each note contained inside this note, formatted using the specified template
^children([template])	includes information from each note descended from this note, formatted using the specified template
^text(note)	includes the text of a specified note
^getFor(note,attribute[,format])	get the value of an attribute for a specified note; if the attribute is a date, the optional format string determines the format of the date.

Tip: Notice that ^children also includes the grandchildren and other descendants of a note, while ^justChildren includes only the immediate children. Most of the time, ^justChildren does what you want. It's far more common to use ^justChildren than to use ^children.

Markup elements that include other notes optionally let you choose an export template to apply. This template might be different from the template normally used to export the note. For example, we might have a set of notes that describe products, with each product description exported on a separate page:

Catalog

Apple cake

Brownie

Brownie (extra dark)

Pear tart

When visitors want to know everything about our apple cake, they'll visit /catalog/AppleCake.html. But, suppose we want to build a list of products – for example, for the navigation sidebar?

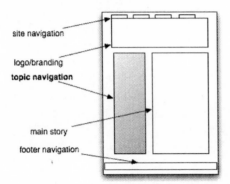

Figure 39. Many sites place topical navigation lists in the sidebar of a page, while presenting site-wide navigation in the header or footer.

We can do this easily. First, we define a template, *Nav Template,* which creates a link to a note:

```
<a href="^URL(this)">^title^</a><br>
```

Now, wherever we want a navigation list to appear, we simply write ^justChildren(Catalog,NavTemplate).

> **Tip**: Tinderbox makes it easy to hide information you don't want to share. You can set **HTMLDontExport** for any note you don't want to export.
>
> For example, some of the children of *Catalog* might represent unannounced future products. Just set **HTMLDontExport**, and ^justChildren will skip over that item.

Relative URLs and ^root^

In the simplest case, each Tinderbox note becomes a Web page. Each, then, has its own unique location on disk, and its own unique URL.

Once you begin to assemble pages from many different notes, though, matters can become more complicated. A note, embedded somewhere on one page, might refer to a note that will be embedded on another page. But that note might be embedded on several different pages! What shall we do?

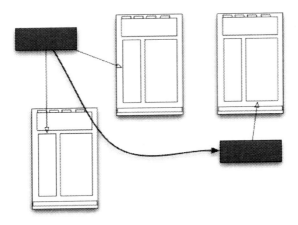

Figure 40. In simple cases, each note has a unique URL. But, when notes are embedded in several places, we may need to tell Tinderbox where we want to link.

The same question may arise when you want to refer to the same URL from many different pages. For example, let's suppose we want to use a stylesheet throughout the site. That's easy: in the <head> of our export template, we link to the stylesheet.

```
<link rel="stylesheet" href="style.css" type="text/css" />
```

This links our note to a stylesheet file called "style.css" that's located in the same directory as this page. But what happens if we want to store the stylesheet in its own directory, say /css/style.css ?

If we know that our exported pages will all be in the top-level directory, we can simply include the appropriate path:

```
<link rel="stylesheet" href="css/style.css" type="text/css"
/>
```

But, if we try to use this from a Web page in another directory, say from /archives/old/myPage.html, then the browser would look for a stylesheet in the wrong place:

Browser looks at: /archives/old/css/style.css

Stylesheet is at: /css/style.css

One solution might be to use fully qualified URLs. These work anywhere, since they aren't relative to the current page.

....href="http://www.mysite.com/css/style.css" ...

Equivalently, we can use root-relative URLs:

....href="/css/style.css" ...

This is simple and reliable, but is not without drawbacks. In particular, it won't work when testing by opening the files on your local disk, since the root of your file system is the top-level disk directory.

Instead, we can use the markup element ^root^, which always gives us the relative path from the current note to the top-level directory.

Path to note	^root^
/note	(nothing)
/archive/note	../
/archive/old/note	../../

In the export template, then, we can link to the stylesheet easily from any subdirectory.

...href="^root^css/style.css"...

Tip: Notice that ^root^ should generally *not* be
followed by a slash. ^root^ emits its own trailing
slash, when needed.

•

11. Composing Print Documents

Exporting Formatted Text

The Nakakoji View exports unformatted text. While you can easily apply suitable styles in your word processor or page layout program, you might sometimes prefer to take advantage of style information from your Tinderbox notes themselves.

This is not to say that you'll want the very same fonts and layouts that you've used in Tinderbox. Generally, you won't. Within Tinderbox, you want to choose fonts that are legible on the screen and comfortable for you to read. When preparing a technical report, an article, or a book, you may need to conform to the publisher's style. In any case, you'll doubtless prefer formats that look good on paper; you have probably already created suitable stylesheets to use in your everyday writing.

In this section, we'll explore one way to build a structured document in Tinderbox, and then export that document to a word processor such as Microsoft Word. The general approach is straightforward:

1. In Tinderbox, we compose the document as a set of notes – often a very large set – inside a single overall container that represents the document.
2. Distinct parts of the document – headings, text sections, figures – are represented as individual notes
3. A prototype represents each element that makes up the document. For example, the prototype •Chapter represents major headings, and the prototype •Section represents minor headings.
4. The entire document container is exported to a single HTML or XML file.

5. The exported file is then opened in your word processor. Using a word processor stylesheet, the text is automatically formatted for print.

The Document Container

Let's begin with a simple Tinderbox outline of a typical document – a school paper, perhaps, or a market research report. We've already used Tinderbox to accumulate notes on the subject, and perhaps at this point we have several hundred individual notes. We may begin by sketching a rapid outline:

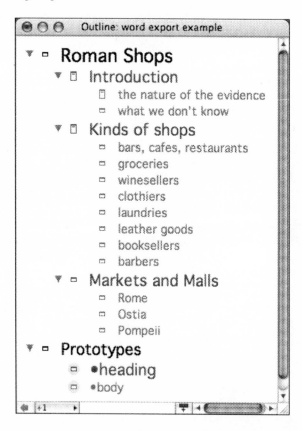

Figure 41. A rapidly sketched Tinderbox outline of our document.

The container **Roman Shops** holds all the notes that will make up our essay. Its template has two very simple jobs:

- provide the framework for the HTML file we plan to construct
- ensure that each note inside **Roman Shops** is exported in turn inside the body of the export file

The export template for Roman Shops is easy to write:

```
<html>
<head> ^title^ </head>
<body>
^justChildren
</body>
</html>
```

The placeholder ^justChildren does precisely what we want: each child of the container will be exported, in turn, at this point in the file.

We'll call this template *Document Template;* only the container document uses it.

The Text Template

Most of the notes in our essay are to be treated as normal body text; they share the prototype named •body and use a very simple template named *Text Template:*

```
^text^
^justChildren
```

We use Document Preferences:HTML Export to make *Text Template* the default template for the entire document.

> **Tip:** If you use HTML Export, your document *must* specify a default template – an export template to be used whenever no specific template is specified. Since all templates a document uses must reside in

the same folder, the default template selects the
folder in which Tinderbox looks for templates.

It's often a good idea to choose a simple template
like *TextTemplate* for a default template. Simple
templates are easier to understand and less likely to
cause confusion.

The Heading Template

If we preferred, we could include headings in the body of the note
texts. But many people prefer to keep the headings separate, making
them more visible in the Tinderbox outline. To make them stand out
even more prominently, we've set the color of the •Headings
prototype to bright red, and set the value of OutlineFontSize to 133,
making the headings 33% larger than other items.

Normally, Tinderbox exports text paragraphs enclosed in <p>...</p>
tags. For heading, though, we prefer different tags:

HTMLFirstParagraphStart: <h2>

HTMLFirstParagraphEnd: </h2>

By changing these attributes in the prototype, we can instantly
arrange for every heading to behave the same way.

The export template for headings is also quite simple: indeed, we
could use *TextTemplate* unchanged. But, in many cases, we'll put the
entire heading in the note title; why type i5 twice?

^if(^get(WordCount)) ^text

^else <h2> ^title^ </h2> ^endif

If we've written a long heading in the note's text, we use the text. If
the text is empty, we find the heading text in the note's title.

Export and Apply Styles

The container **Roman Stores** will now export the entire document. Open its HTMLView and you'll see that the placeholder ^children has been replaced by the contents of all the notes inside **Roman Stores**.

Since we don't want to make separate files for each heading and section within the essay, turn off **Export children as pages.**

We can now export **Roman Stores** to HTML and import the newly created file into our customary word processor or page layout program. For example, we might drop the HTML file on Microsoft Word. In Word, the headings will automatically adopt the **Heading 2** style, while the body text will be assigned to the **Normal (Web)** style.

We can now attach a stylesheet by choosing **Templates and Add-ins...** from the Microsoft Word Tools menu.

12. Sharing Notes: Writing Weblogs

Most of our notes are primarily made for our own use – for later reference, or perhaps simply to work out our own ideas. At times, though, we want to share notes with colleagues and collaborators, with friends, or even with the general public.

Through most of history, reaching a broad audience has required great expense. As recently as the early 20th century, the most cost-effective way to share a written draft with ten or twenty associates involved preparing a formal manuscript, setting that manuscript in lead type, and then printing a pamphlet or volume. The investment of so much time and expense dictates formality and requires care and planning; when so many workers (compositors, press operators, binders) need to be involved (and paid), sharing cannot be undertaken lightly.

The development of offset printing began to change this equation, xerography made a still greater difference, and then the advent of the internet and the Web transformed the economics of information sharing. Sharing a lengthy text or an album of pictures among dozens or thousands of interested people now requires a few moments and a handful of pennies. A child can email their stories to instructors, parents, friends and relatives with a speed and ease that would have made Kipling and Conrad envious.

When we want to share some notes among specific people, we can email copies to them. When the range of recipients is open or indeterminate, or when some recipients might not want to interrupt their work to read our message, we are better off placing the material on the Web at a known address, from which anyone who is interested can retrieve it.

Easy sharing leads naturally to the **weblog**, which collects our notes in reverse-chronological order. Since the newest notes appear first, frequent readers can immediately determine what is newest. At the same time, by preserving older notes, weblogs create an enduring body of notes we (and our readers) can consult at need, and to which we can link whenever we wish.

> My own weblog can be found at
> http://markBernstein.org. It is made with Tinderbox.

Tinderbox and Weblogs

Tinderbox's flexible export tools are ideal for writing and publishing weblogs and other ambitious personal information spaces. Casual sharing, to be sure, can be arranged with many different tools, including free and advertising-supported products that are readily available and easy to use. Tinderbox, on the other hand, is designed to meet the most demanding needs of researchers, journalists, and writers.

> Writing a weblog is serious business. The investment of writing time involved in crafting even a simple weblog is, in the long run, very substantial indeed: if you spend 15 minutes a day writing a short weblog post, that adds up to some 90 hours of work each year. Even a modest weblog can add up to an investment, in kind, of several thousand dollars a year. Though the direct expenditure for software and hosting services is slight, the indirect cost of the writer's time and skill is far from negligible.

How does Tinderbox support serious weblog writing? First, of course, **Tinderbox encourages and facilitates notetaking**. It's easy to add a note to Tinderbox whenever an idea strikes you, and it's easy to refine and revise that note as time and inclination allow.

Second, **Tinderbox is a personal content management assistant**. Every note is automatically tagged with metadata – the time of its creation, the time when it was most recently changed, and so forth. In addition, Tinderbox's elegant **export templates** let you design pages to look however you wish while automatically gathering dozens or even hundreds of notes to include on the page. For example, containers can easily sort their contents in reverse chronological order, automating the selection and arrangement of weblog posts.

Tinderbox **agents can easily create a powerful and intelligent topic and tagging system.** A continuing challenge to weblogs has been finding more effective ways to bring old writing to the attention of people who need to see it. Often, writers assign retrieval tags, keywords, or topics to posts in order to facilitate indexing and retrieval. Tinderbox agents can use these hand-assigned posts *and can assign tags themselves, as needed,* in order to help maintain a category system with less dependence on consistent assignment.

Tinderbox **macros** are also invaluable for weblog writers, making it easy to include complex HTML markup sometimes needed to interface with Web services – bookstore affiliate programs, photograph sharing sites, comment aggregators, social software tools, or bookmark managers.

When exporting a document in HTML, **Tinderbox only updates those pages that have changed** since the previous export. As a result, only the changed files need to be transferred to the Web server. Modern internet file transfer tools will handle this synchronization automatically. Tinderbox can also export directly to WebDAV servers such as Apple's *iDisk,* making web site updates essentially transparent.

Ten Tips for Writing Weblogs[1]

Some parts of the Web are finished creations – unchanging, as polished and as fixed as books or posters. But many parts change all the time:

---

[1] This section originally appeared, in slightly different form, in the 16 August 2002 issue of *A List Apart.* http://www.aListApart.com/stories/writeLiving/

- news sites bring up-to-the-minute developments, ranging from breaking news and sports scores to reports on specific industries, markets, and technical fields
- weblogs, journals, and other personal sites provide a window on the interests and opinions of their creators
- corporate weblogs, wikis, knowledge banks, community sites, and workgroup journals provide share news and knowledge among co-workers and supply-chain stakeholders

Some of these sites change every week; many change every day; a few change every few minutes.

Every revision requires new writing, new words that become the essence of the site. Living sites are only as good as today's update. If the words are dull, nobody will read them, and nobody will come back. If the words are wrong, people will be misled, disappointed, infuriated. If the words aren't there, people will shake their heads and lament your untimely demise.

1. WRITE FOR A REASON

Write for a reason, and know why you write. Whether your daily updates concern your work life, your hobbies, or your innermost feelings, write passionately about things that matter.

To an artist, the smallest grace note and the tiniest flourish may be matters of great importance. Show us the details, teach us why they matter. People are fascinated by detail and enthralled by passion; explain to us why it matters to you, and no detail is too small, no technical question too arcane.

Bad personal sites bore us by telling us about trivial events and casual encounters about which we have no reason to care. Don't tell us what happened: tell us why it matters. Don't tell us your opinion: tell us why the question is important.

If you don't really care, don't write. If you are a student and everybody is talking about exams and papers and you simply don't care, let it be. If your job bores you, it will bore us. (If you despise your job with a rich, enduring passion, that's another thing entirely!)

If your site represents a business or an organization, you must still convey passion and excitement and personality. Your writing need not be informal, but your voice must be clear and direct: impersonal, buzzword-laden double-talk will convince no one. Whether you represent an investment bank or a neighborhood political action group, you need to understand why your message matters. If you do not understand why your product is compelling or comprehend the beauty of your enterprise, find the reason or find a new writer.

Write honestly. Don't hide, and don't stop short. When writing about things that matter, you may be tempted to flee to safe, familiar havens: the familiar, the sentimental, the fashionable. Try to find the strength to be honest, to avoid starting the journey with passion and ending it with someone else's tired formula. The work may be hard, it may be embarrassing, but it will be true – and it will be *you*, not a tired formula or an empty design. And if you can be satisfied with that tired formula, you aren't writing for a reason.

Never, for any consideration, publish a statement you know to be false.

Though you write with passion about things that matter greatly, always remember that it's a big world, filled with people and stories. Don't expect the world to stop and listen. Never expect any individual (or, worse, any quantity of individuals) to read your work, for they may have other things to do. At the same time, steel yourself to anticipate an unexpected visitor, an uninvited guest; the most unlikely people may read your work. Your mother, who never uses a computer, may read your intimate weblog one day in the Library. To be honest with the world, you may need to be honest with your mother; if you cannot face your mother, perhaps you are not ready to write.

2. WRITE OFTEN

If you are writing a weblog, you must write consistently. You need not write constantly, and you need not write long, but you must write often. One afternoon in grad school, I heard B. F. Skinner remark that fifteen minutes a day, every day, adds up to about one book every year, which he suggested was as much writing as anyone should indulge in. You don't need to write much, but you must write, and write often.

If you don't write for a few days, you are unfaithful to the readers who come to visit. Missing an update is a small thing – rudeness, not betrayal – and readers will excuse the occasional lapse.

If you are inconsistent, readers will conclude you are untrustworthy. If you are absent, readers will conclude you are gone. It's better to keep religiously to a once-a-week, or once-a-fortnight schedule, than to go dark mysteriously.

If you cannot write for a time, and the reason for your absence is interesting, write about it. Your honeymoon, your kidney transplant, your sister's gubernatorial inauguration – all these can be predicted and worked into the fabric of your writing so that the interruption, when it comes, seems natural. But avoid, if you can, sudden cryptic pronouncements: "I'll be unable to post for a while" gives us nothing we can use or learn from.

Don't assume that you will find something to say every morning. The day will come, sooner or later, when you need inspiration and find you have none. Store topics, news items, entire articles for slow times. Carry a notebook or a PDA and jot down reminders. You cannot have too many notes saved up, but you can easily find yourself with too few.

Since you write often, use good tools. Select them to fit your hand and voice. Learn to use them well.

3. WRITE TIGHT

Omit unnecessary words.

Choose a visual design that fits your voice. Unless the design is the point of your site, select colors and visual elements that support without dominating. Resist the temptation to add features, for it is often best to use those few technical and design elements that support your mission. Don't rush to replace a good design just because *you* are bored with it: your readers might not appreciate a change.

Read your work. Revise it. Don't worry about being correct, but take a moment now and then to think about the craft. Can you choose a better word – one that is clearer, richer, more precise? Can you do without a word entirely?

4. MAKE GOOD FRIENDS

Read widely and well, on the Web and off, and in your Web writing take special care to acknowledge the good work and good ideas of other writers. Show them at their best, pointing with grace and respect to issues where you and they differ. Take special care to be generous to good ideas from those who are less well known, less powerful, and less influential than you.

Weblog writers and other participants in the living Web gain readers by exchanging links and ideas. Seeking to exchange links without ideas is vulgarly known as blogrolling. Begging high-traffic pages or famous writers to mention you is bothersome and unproductive

Instead of begging, find ways to be a good friend. All writers thrive on ideas; distribute them generously and always share the credit. Be generous with links. Be generous, too, with your time and effort; A-list sites may not need your traffic, but everyone can use a hand.

Many prominent web writers travel a lot – to conferences, meetings, trade shows. Sooner or later, they'll come to your corner of the world. Offer to feed them. Invite them to parties. Offer to introduce them to interesting people. They might be too busy. They might be too shy. But the road can be a lonely place, and it's always interesting to meet interesting, thinking people.

Small, thoughtful gifts are nice. Share books you love, or that you've written. If you're a photographer or an artist, prints and sketches can be unique and memorable. (Include permission to reproduce them on the Web.) Join their cause. Donate to their charity.

Friends are vital for business sites as well, but business and friendship can be a volatile mix. Your prospects, customers and vendors are obvious friends, but both they and your readers will understand that your friendship is not disinterested. Unlikely friends, including your competitors, may prove more convincing.

5. FIND GOOD ENEMIES

Readers love controversy and learn from debate. Disagreement is exciting. Everyone loves a fight, and by witnessing the contest of competing ideas we can better understand what they imply.

Dramatic conflict is an especially potent tool for illuminating abstract and technical issues, whether in software engineering or business planning. At times, choosing a communications protocol or adopting an employee benefits plan may seem an abstract task, barely related to the human crises that daily confront us. If each alternative has a determined, effective advocate, however, it may reveal the source of the conflict and remind us of the consequences of the choice.

To make an abstract or difficult point more real, identify and respond to an advocate who holds a different position. Choose your opponent with care. If you choose a rival who is much less powerful than you, readers may see you as a bully. If your rival is a business competitor, you may seem unscrupulous. The best enemy, in fact, is often a friend – a writer you cite frequently and who often cites you, but with whom you disagree on a specific question.

A handful of individuals seemingly live for controversy and seek out ways to create and inflame disputes. These so-called trolls are chiefly the bane of discussion groups but occasionally find their way into the Living Web. Never engage them; you cannot win. (Trolls, when ignored, will usually retire. If they cause danger or damage that cannot be ignored, the police and the courts will assist you.)

When beginning a debate, always have in mind a plan for ending it. Ill-planned arguments can drag on, lost in a mass of boring detail or irrelevant side-issues. Worse, the personalities of the advocates may become more engaging than the issues, obscuring your purpose entirely. Have in mind, from the outset, an idea of how long you want to engage the issue and how you expect the exercise to end (or reach a resting point). Plan a conclusion before firing the first salvo. You might devise an event – a final meeting, a live debate or online poll – that will provide a sense of closure. Write a joint communique for your readers or your management, summarizing the outstanding issues and highlighting progress. Then archive both sides of the exchange – perhaps with annotation from a neutral authority – so future readers may enjoy and benefit from the conflict.

When it's over, try to make good friends with good enemies.

6. LET THE STORY UNFOLD

Weblogs unfold in time, and as we see each daily revelation, we experience its growth as a story. Your arguments and rivalries, your ideas and your passions: all of these grow and shift in time, and these changes become the dramatic arc of your Web site.

Understand the storyteller's art and use the technique of narrative to shape the emerging structure of your living site. Hint at future events and expected interests: your vacation, the election campaign, the endless midnight hours at work in the days before the new product ships. Surprise with an unexpected flash of humor or a sudden change of direction. Use links within your work to build depth, for today's update will someday be your own back story.

People are endlessly fascinating. Write about them with care and feeling and precision. Invented characters, long a staple of newspaper columnists, are rarely seen on the living Web; an imaginary friend could be a valuable addition to your site, a counterbalance to your own character.

When the star of the site is a product or an organization, temper the temptation to reduce the narrative to a series of triumphs. Although you don't usually want to advertise bad news, your readers know that every enterprise faces challenges and obstacles. Consider sharing a glimpse of your organization's problems: having seen the challenge, your readers will experience your success more vividly.

Interweave topics and find ways to vary your pacing and tone. Piling tension on tension, anger on rage, is ultimately self-defeating; sooner or later, the writing will demand more from you than you can give and the whole edifice will collapse in boredom or farce. When one topic, however important, overshadows everything else in your site, stop. Change the subject; go somewhere new, if only for a moment. When you return, you and your readers will be fresher and better prepared.

7. STAND UP, SPEAK OUT

If you know your facts and have done your homework, you have a right to your opinion. State it clearly. Never waffle, whine, or weasel.

If you are not sure you are right, ask yourself why you are writing. If you are seeking information or guidance from your readers, make it clear that you want to hear from them: invite them to respond. Don't bore them (and discredit yourself) with a hesitant, unformed opinion. If you are writing in order to discover your mind or to try out a new stance, continue by all means – but file the note in your desk drawer, not on your Web site.

If you believe you are right, say so. Explain why. It doesn't matter that you are young, or unknown, or lack credentials, or that crowds of famous people disagree. Don't hesitate or muddy the water. The truth matters; show us the right answer, and get out of the way.

Never lie about your competitors, and never exult in your rival's bad news.

Try, if you can, to avoid inflicting unnecessary pain and humiliation on those who are mistaken. People err, and you, too, may be wrong tomorrow. Civility is not mere stuffiness; it can be the glue that lets us fight for our ideas and, once we recognize the right answer, sit down together for drinks and dinner.

8. BE SEXY

Sex is interesting. Sex is life, and life is interesting. The more of yourself you put into your writing, the more human and engaging your work will be.

If your writing is a personal journal, and if it is honest, you will have to write about things that you find embarrassing to describe, feelings you might not want to share, events that you wouldn't mention to strangers (or, perhaps, to anyone). Decide now what you will do, before it happens.

Undressing, literally, figuratively, or emotionally, has always been a powerful force in personal sites and weblogs. Pictures don't matter in the long run; what matters is the trajectory of your relationship with the reader, the gradual growth of intimacy and knowledge between you.

9. USE YOUR ARCHIVES

When you add something to the living Web and invite others to link to your ideas, you promise to keep your words available online, in their appointed place, indefinitely. Always provide a permanent location (a "permalink") where each item can be found. Do your best to ensure that these locations don't change, breaking links in other people's Web sites and disrupting the community of ideas.

The promise to keep your words available need not mean that you must preserve them unchanged. In time, you may find errors you want to correct. The world changes, and things that once seemed clear may require explanation.

Today, this permanent location is often a chronological archive, a long list of entries for a particular week or month. These archives are useful and easy to make. Many popular tools build chronological archives automatically. But chronological archives are limited: you might someday want to know what you wrote in May of 1999, but why would anyone else care? Topical summaries and overviews are much more helpful to new readers and to regulars alike, and if they require a modest additional effort every day, that effort pays dividends that grow as your archives expand.

Topical archives are Google's natural friend. Remember that your old pages will often be read by visitors from search engines; introduce yourself on every page, and be sure that every page, however obscure, has links to tell people:

> - who you are, what you want, and why you're writing

> - your email address

> - where to find your latest writing

Link to work you've already written – especially to good work that you wrote long ago. Don't be shy about linking to yourself: linking to your own work is a service, not self-promotion.

10. RELAX

Don't worry too much about correctness: Find a voice and use it. Most readers will overlook, and nearly all will forgive, errors in punctuation and spelling. Leave Fowler and Roget on the shelf, unless they're your old friends. Write clearly and simply and write quickly, for if you are to write often you must neither hesitate or quibble.

Don't worry about the size of your audience. If you write with energy and humor about things that matter, your audience will find you. Do tell people about your writing, through short personal email notes and through postcards and business cards and search engines. Enjoy the audience you have, and don't try to figure out why some people aren't reading your work.

Don't take yourself too seriously.

Do let your work on the living Web flow naturally from your passion and your play, your work life and your life at home. Establish a rhythm, so your writing comes naturally and your readers experience it as a natural part of their day or their week. But if the rhythm grows onerous, if you find yourself dreading your next update or resenting the demands of your readers, if you no longer relish your morning Web routine or your evening notetaking, find a new rhythm or try something else. Change the schedule, or voice, or tone. Switch topics. Try, if you can, to resist the temptation to drop things entirely, to simply stop.

Don't worry about those who disagree with you, and don't take bad reviews to heart. The Web is filled with caring and kindness, but thoughtless cruelty can and does cloud every writer's spirit from time to time. Ideas matter, but name-calling doesn't, and petulant critics wrap tomorrow's virtual fish.

13. Sharing Notes: Weblogs and Cheese Sandwiches

Much early writing about weblogs – especially on the literary and journalistic merits and shortcomings of weblogs – was fundamentally wrongheaded. Too often, journalists tried to compare weblogs to established media, seeking to identify whether weblogs could compete with or even replace books and periodicals. But weblogs are not newspapers or novels; these personal information spaces serve different needs and strive toward different ends.

Those who wish to see in weblogs a populist writing revolution are able to find good news in the sheer numbers of people who share their notes through the Web. Those who wish to find evidence of depravity and decadence are able to confirm their expectations as well, as many weblogs (like many books and numerous newspapers) are hastily assembled and poorly written.

Journalists who have argued against attaching importance to weblogs have repeatedly observed that many weblog posts appear dully quotidian, that weblog writers seem to concern themselves with small and unimportant matters.

"I ate a cheese sandwich."

In some cases, this criticism is unfair. Weblogs permit grandmothers and small children to share their notes with their loved ones, and matters of little moment to a stranger are urgently fascinating within the family. Weblogs create a forum for these intimate moments that we may share; and having invited ourselves to read a young person's notes, it seems unjust to denounce their immaturity. Some books and journals have always addressed topics that many find obscure; if sufficient readers can be found to justify the publication of books about picosecond lasers, Klingon etymology, or vernacular Italian poetry, why should we complain? Even should we happen to find these topics uninteresting or opaque, other readers find the books worthwhile. We are not obligated to read them.

Yet the cheese sandwich weblog post cannot, I think, be attributed exclusively to incompetent writing or to the special interests of small communities of which we ourselves are not a part. Understanding the cheese sandwich can, I believe, help us to understand the distinctive nature of weblogs.

What is a Good Weblog?[2]

"The ultimate aim of all creative activity is the web site!"

These words sound preposterous to us. Why? They are, after all, simply a reflection of the core of the Bauhaus manifesto:

Das Endziel aller bilderischen Tätigkeit ist der Bau!

The ultimate aim of all creative activity is the building.

Gropius claimed that the building was the ultimate artistic activity because it draws on so many arts – sculpture and pottery for form, painting for color and tone, engineering for stability and economy – and because it serves people so broadly. The Bauhaus Manifesto foreshadows net culture, and the essential Bauhuas point is that we should expend care and thought everywhere, even in trades traditionally tied to working people and even when working on

---

This section is based on a lecture delivered at the opening of *BlogHui* in Wellington, New Zealand, March 2006.

things that are not necessarily rare and precious. Even the doorknobs should be carefully thought through.

The website draws on engineering and art, too. Web design calls upon our sense of visual composition and color, on painting and graphic design, on planning and economics. Writing for the Web touches on all the literary arts and the social graces. Surely, the ultimate aim of creative activity is now this virtual space, this intellectual network we all inhabit, not the bricks and glass that real-estate brokers buy and sell.

THE ROMANTIC VIEW OF WEBLOGS

Why, then, did Gropius found a revered institution and movement on this grand artistic claim, while we self-deprecatingly regard our Web work as the province of geeks and nerds, as a mere hobby or marketplace? The rhetoric of weblogs, in particular, discusses inclusiveness above all else: weblogs are easy and cheap, they require no special skill to create, and millions of people now have weblogs. Bloggers are *amateurs* who require "friendly" software that is free (or nearly free), intuitive, and accessible.

We treat the weblog writer, in other words, as a child.

On the rare occasions when we have discussed the craft of weblog writing, the rhetoric again emphasizes ease and effortlessness. The key lesson for weblog writers, in this view, seems to be naturalism and authenticity.

> *The more your weblog reflects your interests and your world view, the stronger your voice will be.... Your singular way of experiencing and interpreting the world is the only thing that distinguishes you from a hundred thousand other webloggers.* – Rebecca Blood, *The Weblog Handbook*

This is the romantic view of weblogs, the belief that the excellent (and therefore successful and popular) weblog is the weblog that authentically mirrors our essential wonderfulness.

Tragedy tells us that our weblogs are the playthings of the Gods, subject to the whims of fate and fortune. Comedy promises that our weblogs can succeed through hard work, struggle, and good fortune. Melodrama warns us that there are bad people and evil forces in the world, and that only through courage and determination can our weblogs overcome their malignity. And Romance assures us that, though weblogs fail everywhere, our weblog will prosper because we, ourselves, are wonderful. Mark Bernstein, *HypertextNOW*

In thinking about weblogs, we seldom talk about commitment, dedication, or skill. But of course, the worthwhile task is always beset with difficulty, and only young children and Management expect that wonderful things are effortless.

WEBLOGS AND JOURNALISM

Journalists have often rejected the romantic view as indulgent and immature. Instead, journalists have naturally gravitated toward audience as a figure of merit: a successful weblog should naturally acquire a large following. Many weblogs, however, have far fewer readers than does a newspaper. Does the lack of a mass audience reflect an underlying triviality inherent to the form? Is it a sign of failure, the adverse judgment of the marketplace?

Weblogs are not newspapers; the physical realities of newspapers – the demands of manufacturing and distributing printed paper – impose specific obligations on newspapers that weblogs need not meet. Weblogs are not cinema; they don't require special projectors or theaters. Weblogs are not broadcast media; they don't require expensive transmitters nor (outside of a few dictatorships) do they require government-issued operating licenses.

Mass journalism, in the form defined at the start of the 20th century by Pulitzer and Hearst and Lord Beaverbrook, depends on audience because it depends on advertising to finance news operations. Because newspaper distribution is indiscriminate, rates are inherently tied to circulation; a larger-circulation paper can spend more on better writers and better reporters, further increasing its advantage in circulation. Ultimately, a single newspaper is bound to take over its ecological niche, and multiple newspapers in one place survive chiefly when divisions of language, ethnicity, politics, or class make the dominant newspaper unpalatable to a substantial part of its potential audience.

Ultimately, circulation matters because newspapers (and broadcast media) require extensive capital to defray the cost of specialized printing equipment and to finance the cost of distributing a new product each day throughout an entire region. Newspapers require a large staff simply to print and deliver the paper each day; the cost of reporting and writing is small compared to all the other functions needed to support the enterprise. Weblogs, on the other hand, require very modest investment, almost all of which is editorial. A small-circulation newspaper is almost certainly struggling beneath the crushing weight of its budget, for circulation is the only way it can pay its staff and its debt service. A weblog with no payroll to meet and no presses to buy, a weblog that may not sell advertising at all, can dispense with broad circulation.

Much has been made of the contrast between weblog writers as amateur reporters on the one hand, and professional journalists on the other. It has often been claimed that weblogs fail to understand and adhere to professional standards of fact-checking and conflict disclosure. This argument supposes that journalism is a profession and that journalists maintain professional standards. That some bloggers have indeed proven to be sensationalist and dishonest should hardly astonish us; the less reputable newspapers have always been partisan, sensational, and dishonest. Comparing the best newspapers to the worst bloggers is foolish, and we are so inured to the absurdity, triviality, and pornography peddled in our worst newspapers that we can easily overlook their existence.

That journalism is a profession, moreover, is a very doubtful proposition. Until very recently, the post of newspaper reporter required limited education or training. Early reporters identified with working men. Many joined trade unions. The hallmark and defining quality of a profession, moreover, is control over qualification for admission and membership. No individual, however powerful, can admit you to the bar or make you a physician, but any newspaper owner (and any middle manager and administrator in their employ) can make you a journalist by hiring you. Thenceforth, however poorly you write and whatever standards you neglect, as long as your employer continues to dispatch your checks you will remain a journalist.

Mass journalism depends on an indirect economy, selling advertising to finance reporting, and using the interest that news generates to provide an audience to advertisers. Bloggers, on the other hand, seldom depend very heavily on advertising. Mass journalism is the work of many hands, while bloggers are often solitary; the mass media need to create a trusted brand, while individual bloggers can strive to develop individual trust. Newspapers and broadcasters need to transfer this trust across a broad spectrum of writers and topics; bloggers, having established a personal relationship, do not require branding.

OF CHEESE SANDWICHES

Journalists have often been baffled by the prominence of mundane, personal events in weblogs. The blogger writes that

> *I ate a cheese sandwich.*

This is not news: people eat cheese sandwiches all the time. This would not belong in a newspaper or a broadcast. Why do topics like this appear so often in weblogs?

We have, I think, often misunderstood the cheese sandwich, in part because we have so seldom inquired into the notion of excellence in the weblog. If we subscribe to the belief that weblogs are romantic, then everything depends on the writer's inherent wonderfulness. We just need an excellent creator. Given that, clarity, sincerity, and authenticity are all that we want or need.

But if we look instead to effort and craft and skill as the source of excellence, then we must ask whether the cheese sandwich serves a purpose, and how it can best play its role. What does the blogger's cheese sandwich mean?

We might begin, quite simply, with an excellent cheese sandwich.

I had a very fine cheese sandwich the other night at AOC, a mild and creamy bleu from a small farmhouse cheesemaker in Minnesota.

Food blogging has been immensely successful and influential, both within the world of blogging and also in the food and service industry. The first decade of the 21st century has seen a revolution in food writing, a new interest in the idea of food and in thoughtful reflection on the experience of preparing and eating it. The value of writing well about food – and about the idea of food, the thought that underlies it – has been a prominent theme of recent years, and the rhythms of the weblog naturally fit the food writer's quotidian concerns.

Alternatively, our focus may be didactic: not the cheese sandwich, but rather the method for choosing, preparing, or consuming it. The Web excels at specialized instructions, and net culture has long reveled in finding ways to encourage individuals to undertake new tasks and new technical challenges. The narrative form of the daily weblog promotes instruction by example, demonstrating the writer's progress from recognizing a task to be undertaken, seeking instruction or guidance, enduring setbacks, and finally attaining resolution in the solution the writer discovered or the wisdom the writer has acquired.

Eating a cheese sandwich might be a notable accomplishment, a turning point in a long narrative.

Despite my desperate illness, in defiance of the effort of disease (or of the Gods) to grind me to dust, today I ate a cheese sandwich.

We are not interested in the cheese any more than we care about Queequeg's harpoon or Lady Windermere's cucumber sandwiches or the recovery of the Maltese falcon. We care about what happens, and the cheese sandwich is merely an artist's pretext for revelation.

The cheese sandwich may serve instead as the conventional occasion for an extraordinary event. Because the mundane is common, we find it everywhere; when writing of extraordinary events or unusual places, we may need to remind the reader that these places and these people, too, are merely places and people. Though they reside far from us, surrounded by strange customs and exotic architecture and (perhaps) extraordinary events, these people see the sun and the moon and they eat lunch.

The cheese sandwich may be a symbol or an emblem, standing concretely for an abstraction. In much of the finest food writing of the 20th century, in M.F.K. Fisher and Elizabeth David and Patience Grey, we see what Adam Gopnick terms the "mystical microcosmic" approach, which

> ... is essentially poetic, and turn[s] every remembered recipe into a meditation on hunger and the transience of its fulfillment... sad thoughts on the love that got away on the plate that time forgot.

A particular cheese sandwich might identify a place and time, situating a story specifically, in order to help us understand and believe in it.

Very often, the cheese sandwich may be an example of a specific grievance or indignity. When we write, for example, of the thin, stale, and unhealthy cheese sandwiches served to the unfortunate inmates in American prisons, we are not speaking merely of cheese, nor is this specific sandwich the focus of our resentment. It is representative, emblematic of other and greater ills. It is a symbol of a situation that demands redress. This use of the cheese sandwich to exemplify deplorable practices has been common in political weblogs, particularly in those written by scholars and experts who provide a window into specialized domains. These may write extensively about a specific event or policy, not only for its own importance but because it represents a spectrum of related issues.

In addition to its primary meaning, a cheese sandwich post may also play a role in narrative pacing. Weblogs, by definition, unfold in time. New posts are added, episodes and characters accumulate.

Sometimes, it is artistically desirable to slow down, to relieve tension or to moderate the pace of events. After a series of exciting or angry posts, we may seek out occasion for a time of calm and repose, a return (perhaps only a brief return) to normalcy or a restatement of the destination to which the writer aspires or the position from which the writer is fleeing.

As we have seen, weblogs can indeed contain a remarkable array of cheese sandwich posts. Far from indicating narcissism or triviality, the cheese sandwich in the hands of a skilled blogger can be used to good effect:

- The excellent cheese sandwich: commonplace or quotidian tasks performed with special care or effectiveness
- Instruction
- The notable accomplishment
- Conventional occasion for an extraordinary event
- Symbol or emblem
- Representative of place and time
- Focus of a larger issue or resentment
- Pacing device

The importance of the cheese sandwich should not surprise us. Even epic is built out of common parts. Hamlet knows that "'tis common; all that live must die, Passing through nature to eternityWhat matters is not the unique gravity of our matter, nor its mass, but the way we use it.

The only end of writing is to enable the readers better to enjoy life, or better to endure it. – Samuel Johnson

PUBLIC, NOBITIC, AND PRIVATE NOTES

A further confusion in weblog criticism arises because the audience for notes varies from one writer to another, and from one time to another, in kind as well as number. Too often, we assume that a good weblog is simply a popular weblog, that the size of the audience reflects its quality (or that would reflect its quality if the world were just).

This misunderstands both the nature of weblogs and the nature of notes. Craft, wit, grace, and insight are not generally measured in terms of traffic or box office receipts.

Some weblogs, indeed, are written in what literary critic Frank Miner called the *public mode*. The author consciously writes for a broad audience, addressing the world and (perhaps) posterity. Other writers adopt the *private mode*, addressing their reflections as if to themselves. Milton stands at a great height and shows us a *Paradise Lost;* Donne lights a candle in the darkness of his private study to sketch a poem addressed to his own soul.

The writer who chooses the private mode may, of course, intend that the work will be read by others, perhaps even by many others. Some writers in the private mode are ambitious for audience, others indifferent, just as some musicians and painters seem to care more deeply than others for broad popularity and general recognition. Modes are a matter of voice and technique, not ambition.

We may also distinguish a third mode, which Miner calls social and which (because "social software" means something else) I will here call *intimate* or *nobitic*. Here, the notional audience lies beyond the author but does not extend to the world at large. Letters intended for publication are *nobitic*. So, too, are stories notionally told among friends or written for our family, *Heart of Darkness* or *Winnie the Pooh*.

We have always recognized that journals and diaries adopt any of these modes. Thoreau's *Journal* is notionally a diary, but clearly it was composed and intended to influence the general public and the electorate. Da Vinci and Pepys, on the other hand, wrote for themselves: Da Vinci wrote in code, and Pepys in an obscure shorthand to which, in the more sensitive amatory passages, he added a further layer of pidgin French and Italian. Other diaries seem fundamentally nobitic: Anne Frank invents the diary as a sort of character she can address because she wants someone outside the family to whom she can complain.

Understanding the distinction between private, nobitic, and public weblogs is crucial to appreciating the craft of these shared notes, and for thinking clearly about what notes should be shared and how those notes can best be expressed. One of the earliest weblogs, Magdalena Donea's *Moments,* begins with the author as a 14-year-old girl on a Romanian hillside:

> *In the winter of 1983, I stood on a barren hillside hundreds of feet above the coast of the Black Sea, and I promised myself that yes, I would take care to record in my mind, and later remember, the time that was to come, each and every moment of it. It was a promise I kept well.* [3]

This declaration announces at once a private and a public ambition: the author wants to (privately) remember, but also plans to share that memory with the weblog's readers. She stands (almostliterally) at the threshold of transition: at the border between her old home and the new world, at the border between the old postwar Europe and the new, and at the boundary between childhood and adult life. The artful mixture between private and public modes, the carefully-contrived confusion of publicized intimacy, has long been a characteristic of weblogs and a source of perplexity to their critics.

Notes are memory made concrete. When we keep Tinderbox notes in order to accumulate research for an article we are writing, we are explicitly aiding our memory. We make a ToDo list so we need not worry that we will overlook important tasks. Other notes remind us what we have done — the books we've read, the movies we'd looked forward to seeing but found instantly forgettable, the dishes we chose for the dinner party last month, the work assignments at last January's project meeting – because we might want this information to be handy in the future. All these are literally *memoranda:* things to be remembered.

Though we write these notes to our future selves, some of them might perhaps be interesting or useful to our intimate friends, our colleagues, or our assistants. When we jot down that we enjoyed a story by Deborah Eisenberg or Philip K. Dick, that jotting might

---

http://moments.kia.net

perhaps be interesting to your family and friends, should they find themselves wondering what you'd enjoy for your birthday. It might also amuse a former student, or a half-forgotten schoolfriend who happened to wonder what interests you now. Your assistants and colleagues might occasionally find the information interesting or useful. An intern who is working in your division might like knowing what sort of things someone like you reads, not least because they are asking themselves whether they want to become someone like you. Your mother might be interested, too.

WRITING FOR MOM

Here we come to the very core of the difference between weblogs and the press: mass-produced media require a mass audience but weblogs do not. Many weblogs have small audiences – some, one suspects, are read only by the writer's mother.

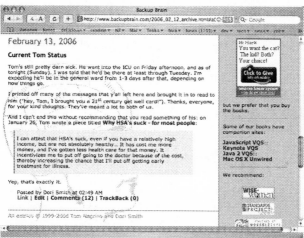

Figure 42. Dori Smith uses her weblog here to keep readers informed of a family crisis. "Tom is still pretty darn sick. He went into the ICU on Friday...." Friends, colleagues, and correspondents in this way can choose to enter the family's intimate circle.

But writing to your mother is not a sign of shameful failure. Writing letters to your mother is generally considered a fine thing to do. No one objects to the idea of sending private electronic mail to one's mother; the difference between email and weblog is here an unimportant detail. Weblog posts cost as little as electronic mail messages; they merely happen to be slightly more accessible to third parties. You can write for your mother, knowing that your sisters, cousins, and aunts might like to read the letter, too. We've always known that Mother might show the letter to Aunt Joan, of course; weblogs simply make it clear that we welcome this kind of intimate sharing.

Sometimes, our notional audience is even smaller: many diaries address a notional reader but their creators neither expect nor want them to be read by any specific reader (and most certainly not by the writer's mother!). Who, for example, could Anne Frank have expected to read her *Diary*? Charlotte Salomon's massive graphic notebooks *Life? Or Theater?* were surely written without much expectation that anyone would see them. Henry Darger never seems to have mentioned his immense, unpublishable fantasies of the *Vivian Girls* to anyone. Artists frequently spend many hours sketching – creating drawings and paintings intended not to be shown but rather to inform the artist's other work and to work through problems of which the artist may, indeed, be only partially aware.

A vast amount of invaluable writing is intended for very modest numbers of readers. Scholarship appeals chiefly to scholars – not simply because it is their business to be interested in scholarship, but because many complex and subtle arguments demand special expertise and extraordinary knowledge from the audience. Scientific and engineering work typically demands familiarity with specialized knowledge of mathematics and of the physical sciences; intricate legal arguments and public policy recommendations, too, may require so much attention and background knowledge as to render them largely inaccessible to a broad readership. Though their audience is small, these specialized works are in fact our most important writing, the writing that announces our finest achievements.

Concern with the "long tail" of small audience weblogs was misplaced. Many weblogs do not and should not care whether their audience is numerous. What matters is whether the weblogs are known to, and read by, those people for whom they are intended and suitable. Political weblogs want to be read by people who shape and

who act upon political opinion. Scientific weblogs want to be read by
the audience of scientists active in their particular specialty. And
when weblogs are written for the writer's immediate friends and
family, what matters most is whether the weblog amuses and
enlightens that family.

14. Why Is Tinderbox So Complicated?

At times, Tinderbox seems large and complex. Tinderbox has notes, containers, agents, aliases, and adornments. Tinderbox offers outlines, maps, charts, treemaps and roadmaps. Tinderbox agents and containers have actions, and notes can have rules. When you export, Tinderbox lets you build export templates using dozens of powerful placeholders.

Tinderbox is a tool for making, analyzing, and sharing notes; in a sense, its main competitor is scrap paper. Tinderbox is more complex than paper. You already know how to use 3x5 cards. Little yellow stickers are less expensive than Tinderbox, and they don't require a computer. Tinderbox, on the other hand, uses all the power of the latest personal computers, and is eager to take advantage of computers many times faster than you can buy today.

Why can't Tinderbox be simpler?

The illusion of complexity

You don't have to use facilities you don't need.

But they have to be ready for you, because someday you will probably need them.

Notes are not simple

We forget how difficult some tasks are, because we do them all the time. Catching a ball. Driving a car. These are hard – we spend years learning how to do them.

We also forget that we might be able to do some things much better than we all do them today. We assume that the limits of what we can do are inherent. But that's just not true.

Within living memory, everyone knew that city streets had to be full of dust and dung. You couldn't feed people without cartage, you couldn't use expensive cars and railroads to haul all the food a city required, and where horses go, manure follows. I'm not elderly, but I can remember occasional cart horses in central Chicago that did real work – not merely hauling tourists. But, today, work horses in American cities are a distant memory because trucks are cleaner, cheaper, and faster.

This also means that the fellow who used to groom the horses has been succeeded by a worker in charge of a complex on-the-road rig with dozens of gears and a state-of-the-art diesel. It's not easy to drive a truck; back in the 1890s, you'd want an engineer in charge of that engine. Now, you just hire a driver. (A few years ago, I took a cab from Boston Logan Airport and learned that the driver's grandfather worked at the Porter Square livery stable.)

Better tools let us do more – especially when they become widely used. Some tools, like the elevator, eventually become so simple that everyone uses them and nobody thinks of them. Some, like the automobile, require lots of training, regulation, and insurance to repair mishaps.

And, as soon as we really understand a new tool, we look beyond to a new horizon. I complain of unnecessary waits at airport security on the way to a tedious flight to New York or London, and rarely think as I contemplate the delays how, not long ago, either trip would have taken a week – or a month.

What could we do with better tools for notes? What would such tools mean?

Why we need it all

Tinderbox has lots of parts. Each part was expensive to build. Each requires constant maintenance in the code, and each requires documentation and training costs. Could we do without some parts?

The exercise of removing parts from Tinderbox helps remind us what each part does.

Aliases. Aliases add flexibility to the document hierarchy, allowing the same note to appear in several places. This encourages information reuse, and avoids distracting indecision when trying to figure out where a particular note should be stored. Aliases are important for agents; if agents made a new copy of each note they found, Tinderbox files might soon grow unwieldy.

Aliases were probably the most expensive component of Tinderbox to implement. In principle, the alias is simple enough. In practice, aliases raise a host of subtle semantic questions. Which attributes inhere in the alias, and which are inherited from the original? When notes are deleted, its aliases are deleted too; what happens if the deletion is undone? How can we read an alias from a file, if its original has not been read yet?

It's not rocket science

Tinderbox was extremely hard to build. Innovative software tends to be small and limited; elaborate commercial software, because it requires so many hands and so much capital, tends to stick to safe and familiar sequels in established categories.

Tinderbox has tens of thousands of lines of code, each of which has to be correct. We worked hard to make sure each line does everything it can, to find ways to reuse the same code in many contexts, We did our best to keep Tinderbox small. It could be smaller, but I don't think it could be *much* smaller.

We also worked hard to polish the user interface where it counts, and to make sure that Tinderbox offers you lots of security and safety. Tinderbox files are reasonably compact; they're easy to back up. Making an extra copy of your notes for safekeeping is a snap. You can read a Tinderbox file yourself, without special tools. Other programs can use them, too. Your data is yours.

Chrome plate, not sterling

We wanted Tinderbox to be accessible to scholars and students, to workers and thinkers. In part, we wanted to do this because it is the right thing to do. But it's also sound business sense: workers and thinkers are the people who need Tinderbox most. But people who work with ideas, in our world, do not always command vast financial resources; Tinderbox needs to be affordable.

Much of today's software is over-engineered, designed for the needs of casual users, newspaper pundits, and venture capital analysts. This makes great sense for other markets, for products that everyone needs to use occasionally. Tax software, for example, and Web shopping applications, may place a heavy emphasis on surface sheen and cater primarily to the needs of infrequent users.

We need to learn to recognize and enjoy software tools built for use.

Why Are Templates Hard?

Tinderbox export templates are flexible and powerful, but they're also very simple. Yet, though some people find templates intuitive, others find them baffling. Why do templates sometimes seem hard? I think two distinct sources of confusion are at work: indirection, and magic.

INDIRECTION

Indirection is one of the key concepts of computer science, one of the handful of big ideas that make computer science an intellectual discipline rather than a bunch of recipes and instruction manuals. Along with a few related concepts like *recursion, data structure,* and *modularity,* indirection is the reason we often expect college students to spend a semester or two learning about computer science.

> Of course, many of us haven't studied much computer science. I didn't; when I was in college, Swarthmore had no computer science department. There were a handful of courses, mostly taught in the engineering program, but I soon learned that part of my night job at the computer center involved helping people figure out their homework assignments. Since I'd already done the homework, there didn't seem much point in taking the courses.
>
> This is much harder to do today, in a more credentialist era. I know lots of older researchers who never studied computers formally and who have degrees in engineering, mathematics, or (like me) in one of the physical sciences. But almost all my younger colleagues got some formal coursework (and a computer science degree) under their belt along the way.

Indirection is one of the beautiful ideas that underpin computer science. It repays study. When a procedure or a document becomes complicated, we can reduce the complexity by referring indirectly to some part of the problem.

Tinderbox revels in indirection:

- Links connect notes to other notes. When either note is moved to a new place in the document, links keep the two connected.
- Aliases connect to places in the Tinderbox document's hierarchy. One object can be in several places simultaneously; each alias refers indirectly to a different place.
- Agent and container actions can establish indirect constraints. For example, we may say that "all notes in this

section must be marked *Urgent* and colored bright red"; an agent can enforce this constraint by scanning the section and ensuring that notes inside it are marked and colored appropriately.

Templates use indirection to compose complex documents and Web pages from many smaller notes. Instead of working with one very large and complex document, as we typically do in a word processor or page layout program, Tinderbox uses templates to assemble complex documents from many smaller, simpler notes.

Recursion

Computer science teachers have found that some students find recursion to be a singularly difficult and disturbing concept. Weeks or months of the introductory computer science curriculum are devoted to teaching students the elements of recursion; because recursion is so powerful and so important to software design, most students will return to study recursion in many forms before they become completely comfortable with it.

Tinderbox outlines are inherently recursive. A note has one parent and may have many children – and each of those children may in turn have many children. People who are completely at home with contemporary computer science will see immediately that exporting this kind of recursive structure is easily done by recursive templates:

> Template name: outline

> ^indent ^title
> ^justChildren(outline)

Occasionally, Tinderbox users will attempt to avoid recursion by creating separate templates for each level of the outline:

> Template name: level3
> ^indent ^title
> ^justChildren(level4)

While schemes like this are entirely possible, they often entail creating lots of nearly identical templates. This burden may, in fact, be welcomed by users who are especially uncomfortable with recursion. Tinderbox permits you to unroll recursive templates in this way, but recursion is probably more concise and easier to maintain.

Magic

The other reason that export templates sometimes seem baffling stems from their simplicity. They're easy to get *almost* right. That makes it tempting, if things aren't quite working, to start tweaking and tinkering without direction, attempting to fix something without really understanding what's going wrong. Sometimes, this works. Often, it's a recipe for confusion.

A further recipe for confusion is found in the attempt to debug an export template (especially one that involves CSS) by examining the way a page looks in a particular Web browser, rather than inspecting the HTML or XML code directly. The HTML View window provides fast and easy access, letting you understand exactly what Tinderbox is doing and compare the result with what you expected to observe. Introducing additional layers of obscurity can only add confusion, since a faulty page layout might have several causes:

- Tinderbox is not exporting information with the expected markup
- The browser does not display the information as you expected because the browser's layout engine is erroneous
- The browser's layout differs from what you expected but conforms to what the browser's designer expected
- The browser is using cached stylesheets instead of the style sheets you wished it to use.

When export templates misbehave, **simplify** the problem as much as possible to **isolate** the issue and to make it more clearly visible. If the problem is not evident, try hand-coding the correct markup; does it operate as you expected? If so, how does it differ from the Tinderbox markup?

> A basic command of HTML is becoming part of the intellectual repertoire of an educated person. You can probably acquire the needed competence in an afternoon or two of study.

15. Meeting Notes

Simple Notes At Simple Meetings

Tinderbox users often build one or more central documents that come to serve as a center of their work life. For example, right now I use at least three Tinderbox documents every day, whatever I'm working on.

- **Projects** holds a large list of tasks and projects. Everything I'm planning to do, and almost everything I'm seriously considering, winds up in Projects. Whenever I promise to review a book or decide to implement a new software feature, the task goes somewhere in Projects.
- **Tinderbox ToDo** is a large planning file that holds every feature, research topic, and marketing concept we want to explore for Tinderbox. Some of these are concrete and urgent, others are sketches for broad research projects that we might not be able to undertake for years.
- **Daybook** is a simple list of notes, one per day, where I record facts I might need again. Whenever I order something, I mention it in the daybook; if, months from now, I realize it never arrived and that I'm no longer certain I ever ordered it, the Daybook will know. Similarly, when I'm not completely sure where I should file something, I mention where I *did* file it in the daybook.

> **Tip:** the original meaning of "memoranda" is, "things to be remembered".

These Tinderbox documents are valuable, but they're also large and complicated. Keeping them fresh and useful requires a measure of *information gardening* (Chapter 15) – weeding out old or irrelevant data, pruning details that are no longer useful, moving items to the place where they truly belong.

Staff meetings, teleconferences, and business lunches are not ideal occasions for information gardening. Instead of trying to work with my key files directly, I often create a fresh little Tinderbox document just to hold notes for the meeting at hand. These simple notes go straight into an outline, and the document is then saved in a special Inbox folder. At the end of the day, I'll sort notes from these *ad hoc* Tinderbox lists and put them where they belong.

Usually, these lists need no advance preparation; I just open Tinderbox and start adding notes. If a meeting promises to be more complicated, though, I might create some containers in advance, and perhaps copy some reminders from my Projects Tinderbox.

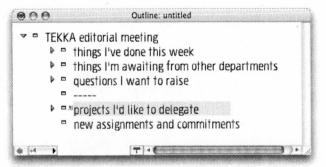

Figure 43. By setting out a few topical containers in advance, I can easily prepare to take notes in meetings as the need arises. Elaborate apparatus is not necessary here, and I can usually anticipate the categories of notes I'm likely to make.

Outlines work well for temporary notes from routine meetings. Because the context is familiar, you can usually anticipate what sort of notes you'll make and how you'd like to arrange them. Should unexpected topics arise, they're easy to accommodate on the fly. Because you know your business, you know what to expect; routine meetings don't require much apparatus.

Major meetings – scholarly symposia, big professional conferences, annual strategy retreats, policy summits – generate larger and less predictable notes.

Trying to take notes for a major meeting in an outline can be an exercise in frustration. When new ideas arise, you need to think about the new ideas – not about where they fit in your outline. For big meetings, we need all our tools.

Preparing for Meetings and Conferences

All-day and multi-day conferences represent a big investment. They occupy hours or days – often as much as a week. They're often expensive to attend. Registration fees are costly, and the cost of travel and lodging are often substantial. The time spent in preparation, in transit, and in attendance represents a big investment as well. These costs all argue for creating more thorough notes, and for sharing them more effectively throughout your organization.

Before the meeting starts, sketch out a fresh Tinderbox framework for your notes. This preparation can help you focus and prepare yourself as well as your Tinderbox; it's a particularly good airplane task.

When attending a research conference, I'm most interested in big pictures and big issues – especially in issues I wasn't expecting. At trade shows, similarly, I'm most interested in unexpected synergies and alliances, not in the announcements I can easily anticipate from companies we already work with. The most productive meetings, I find, are often those outside my immediate field, conferences in tangential areas where I may discover unexpected connections. But because I don't know the field, I can't make an outline in advance; instead, I do most of our notetaking in the Tinderbox map view.

To begin, I divide up the (empty) map space into four thematic quadrants:

Figure 44. Conceptual overview of a conference map. Reserve space in advance for thinking about the big picture (top-right) and for keeping track of details (top-left).

At the top of the map, make an adornment to reserve space for notes about common themes, opinions, and interests that span sessions. These themes may not appear on the program, and often they are not the topics that the meeting organizers anticipated. A conference may be titled "Widgets: A Century of Progress" many months or years in advance, but the central topic will often turn out to be a new discovery or unexpected legal, political, or financial development that arose only weeks or days earlier. Gaining a better understanding of these overarching issues and sentiments is often the main reason you attend meetings; you may be able to find out what people *said* by reading the Proceedings, but for a good sense of what they're thinking and feeling and anticipating, you may need to be there.

At the same time, you'll need to reserve some space to keep track of logistics and plans that the meeting provokes. The left quadrant of your Tinderbox map gives you a simple, accessible places to jot down ideas for things to do (or think about) during the meeting, or to act on soon after returning home. These might include:

- Questions you want to ask a speaker – especially questions better asked off-stage

- People you particularly want to meet, or invite to lunch or dinner
- People who have done you a favor, whom you'll want to thank after the meeting
- Experiments suggested by presentations
- Books to purchase, Web sites to visit, products to locate and explore
- People you met whom you want to remember as possible collaborators, customers, or potential employees
- Meals, parties, and other auxiliary events you might want to attend
- Ideas for improving your notetaking, and planning for future conferences and meetings

I usually reserve the top-left quadrant for conceptual planning, and the bottom-left quadrant for plans and contacts to be made right away. Notes about questions I'd like to ask right away, or references I want to look up during the next break, go at the left edge of the map; tasks I want to consider when I return home can be placed further away, at the top-left corner.

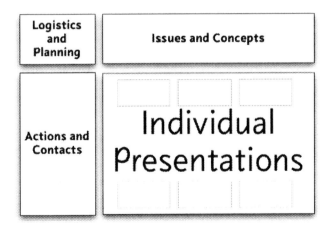

Figure 45. In practice, most of the map is reserved for details of individual sessions. By reserving space in advance for more general notes, we can make sure the mass of detail doesn't overwhelm the general picture.

While laying these foundations, I also like to set up Tinderbox preferences that make notes more comfortable to read, and less distracting to write, in a crowded auditorium or unfamiliar conference room.

Map Background Color: I choose a fresh background color for each conference. First, this lets me know right away that I'm working in the right Tinderbox file. (I sometimes need to refer to other Tinderbox files during a meeting, especially during controversial panels. I don't want to accidentally start adding notes to last year's file!)

If the meeting is likely to be held in an auditorium or theater, choose a darker background color than you might otherwise prefer. Laptop screens can be distracting beacons in a dark room.

Map Font. If you have been using Tinderbox for years, your default Map Font might be the old standby, Geneva. Try a cleaner and more legible sans serif font. I enjoy Optima, Eurostile, Futura, or Lucida Grande among many others.

A legible script font – P22 Eaglefeather, say, or David Siegel's Tekton – can be a pleasantly informal alternative.

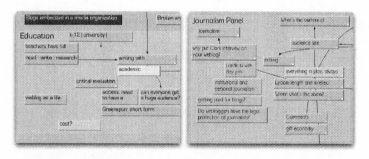

Figure 46. Sections of two maps from the same conference use different fonts to distinct effect. Left: Eurostile. Right: P22 Eaglefeather.

When a meeting is likely to offer a lively mixture of fact and opinion, I sometimes use different fonts to emphasize the distinction.

Figure 47. Using an informal handwritten font – especially a very legible one – can help distinguish fact from opinion. Use prototypes to make it easier to create different kinds of notes quickly. Fonts: Lucida Grande, Immi 505 (Linotype)

Plan for sharing: You'll often want to increase the map font size for legibility. First, you may want to show some of your raw notes to colleagues back at the office; your maps, projected on a conference room screen, will make a more effective presentation if the fonts are large and clear.

Realistically, your neighbors at the conference are bound to find your notes intriguing. Accept that people *will* look over your shoulder; legibility helps assure them that you're paying attention to the same speaker, not reading your email or doing office work.

Color Scheme: I prefer to define one or two special note colors for each conference, choosing hues that blend well with the map background color. Bold color schemes grow tiring after a long day, and less contrast between notes and the background helps call attention to the note labels.

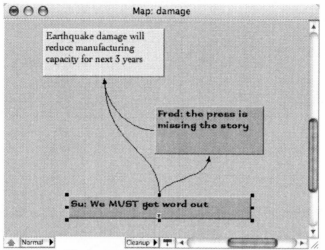

Figure 48. In this document, I've redefined "black" to a light gray. Other colors, too, are lighter and more neutral. "Red" doesn't have to be a fire engine.

Prototypes: On the road, keep your note environment simple. Complexity can be distracting, and a five-minute interruption that might be innocuous in your office could lead you to miss a crucial announcement at a meeting.

Still, I like to set up a few Tinderbox prototypes in advance for special kinds of notes. These prototypes assign distinctive appearance to notes, so they stand out clearly in the map, and also help keep related notes tied together for later analysis. Prototypes I often use include:

- Contact information: a distinctive style reminds me to record who is speaking and jot down information I'll need to locate them later.
- Questions: Again, making questions stand out lets you scan them quickly, helping you choose what to ask about when you get the opportunity.
- Resources: Some notes merely document references and resources that provide additional evidence or background. I like to choose style and shape to make these fade into the background until needed, freeing me to concentrate on the

issues but still providing a good place to record notes you might need later.

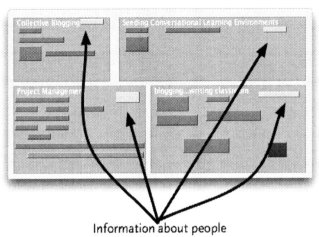

Information about people

Figure 49. The distinctly colored note in the right-hand corner of each session holds contact information for speakers and panelists.

Agents and Actions: I seldom use many agents in conference notes, but a handful of agents can provide handy on-the-fly analysis. *Keyword agents* simply search for notes that contain words of special interest to you. An agent that gathers all mentions of your own project, for example, can be handy. If, during the conference, I notice that several speakers are picking up on a common theme or sharing a new buzzword, I often add an agent that tracks this emerging meme through the rest of the meeting.

Make adornments sticky. Adornments are simple background elements that help clarify map relationships like those proposed in Figure 45. Adornments are always layered behind your notes, and help define spaces the notes inhabit.

If an adornment is *sticky*, moving the adornment also moves all the notes that lie on it. Sticky adornments are a tremendous help in reorganizing your notes on the fly, especially when you discover that you need more space in part of the map.

During the meeting, I often make crowded adornments *sticky*, so they will be easy to reposition. When an adornment is uncomfortably full or when I need to make space for a new topic, I can quickly drag the crowded adornment out of the way. Later, I usually turn *sticky* off making it easier to fine-tune the position of adornments.

Images: A digital camera can serve two valuable roles in a meeting. It's important (but all too rare) that you understand these roles and keep them separate.

First, you'll want to take some pictures of the meeting venue, its environs, and of the people who attended the meeting as an aide-mémoire. For these pictures, atmosphere and mood matter much more than detail. Take a few pictures during your journey to the meeting, including highway or airport shots. Get exterior pictures of the meeting place, as well as pictures of attendees in session and during breaks and meals; your goal in these pictures is to capture the locale and the mood, not to grab candid photos of famous people rushing back to their hotel rooms.

> **Tip**: Try not to use flash in the auditorium. Flash is ineffective unless you're within ten or twenty feet of the subject, so it's not going to improve the picture. But flash *is* very distracting for speakers – and for people sitting nearby.

Second, keep a digital camera handy for capturing pictures of complex visuals. Technical presenters sometimes overload a single slide with a wealth of data; if this data is important to you, you may find yourself so wrapped up in copying it down that you can't follow the ideas of the talk. When this happens, just take a picture of the screen: it won't make an *attractive* photograph, but you'll be able to review the visual at leisure, freeing you to concentrate on the rest of the presentation.

After The Meeting

The most important role that notetaking plays in an important meeting and conference should be focus: helping you attend to the most important aspects and issues. Once the meeting is over, that role is essentially complete, but your notes can provide lasting value in other ways.

First, review all your notes shortly after the meeting. Long plane trips home can be a good time for a thoughtful, relaxed consideration. Alternatively, schedule an appointment with yourself about one week after you return from the meeting, and spend half an hour simply reviewing the meeting. This review will help consolidate your impressions and remind you of unanswered questions and unfinished tasks that arose during the conference.

Even if you are not required to write a trip report as part of your job, consider preparing a simple report for your co-workers and colleagues. You might consider posting the report on your Web site or weblog, or sending it to a newsletter or to the conference organizers.

> **Tip**: In academe and in technical fields, trip reports from graduate students and junior researchers are particularly valued by the entire community. More prominent members of the field can rarely write reports; not only are they busy, but their opinions are so widely known, and they serve on so many committees, that any expression of opinion may cause surprise or offense. Writing and publishing thoughtful conference reports can be a very effective route to introduce yourself to the broader research community.

When drafting a trip report, try to avoid a narrowly chronological account. After the conference is over, nobody cares what happened on Thursday morning. Instead, try to focus on important results and notable ideas from the top quadrant of your notes, using these to introduce specific details from the bottom section.

> **Tip**: Use snapshots of the venue and the attendees to carry the narrative story of the conference and meeting. This is why you took pictures of the journey to the conference and of the conference venue itself, Keep the images small – they might not require captions if their role is clear.

Keep all your old meeting notes together in a special folder, and keep them indefinitely. Because Tinderbox files are fairly compact, you needn't worry about the cost of keeping an extra copy or two around.

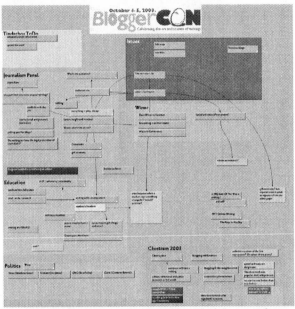

Figure 50. Bloggercon I meeting notes. Interdisciplinary conferences often cover a lot of ground and head in unexpected directions. Fortunately, you can always expand the Tinderbox map.

After the meeting, you may also find it useful to reorganize your notes. Looking back at the entire conference, you will likely perceive new relationships and fresh associations. Record these now, because these relations may be less clear to you later. Some notes that seemed worth recording but which had no obvious place can now find their home. Other notes may now seem relevant in several places; make aliases or adjust their map position to make this clear.

You may also find it helpful at this point to sweep related notes into topical containers. Containers make it harder to see relationships between items outside the container, but they also help focus your attention; if the overall map seems cluttered and complex, try adding some containers.

Tip: work with a copy of the file, not with your original notes, when trying a radical reorganization.

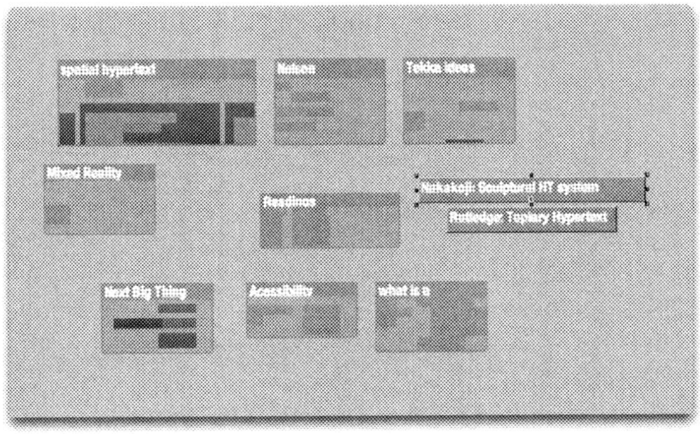

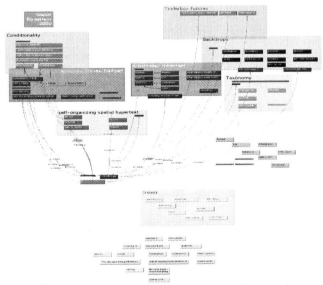

Figure 51. When the meeting topic is familiar, a more systematic and hierarchical note style may be warranted. Conference notes on Hypertext '03.

Figure 52. For a freeform discussion or technical workshop, a large map provides a flexible but ordered workspace. Third Spatial Hypertext Workshop, 2002.

Informal Presentations

You can easily rework a copy of your notes to form a flexible and effective presentation to brief coworkers on your return.

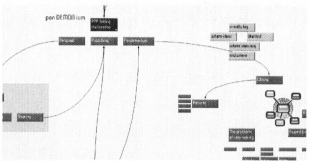

Figure 53. Part of a presentation map, Personal Publishing Pandemonium, Maastricht, 2002.

The most common business tool for presentations today is PowerPoint®, which is modeled after the process for creating 35mm photographic slides used by lecturers a generation ago. PowerPoint, used with care and judgment, can make elegant and useful slides. Used in haste, it invites disaster. Worse, PowerPoint presentations are often hard to revise, while your presentation may need to change at the last moment. Volatility is characteristic of business — and agility is especially useful in important, informal presentations.

> **Exercise**: What does it cost your organization to send a technical employee to a single conference? Be sure to include ancillary costs. Don't forget the employee's salary and benefits – and the staff and management time required to secure approvals and process expense reports. Also, compute the cost of the employee's conference report, including the salary and benefits of everyone who attends the presentation or reads the trip report.
>
> Reporting is expensive, but it's the only mechanism for spreading the benefits of the meeting throughout the organization.

When preparing your notes for a presentation, consider the Tinderbox presentation map as a large blackboard. Use a clear, legible font in **text windows** to expand points that require detail, and use links to draw the eye from one topical region to another.

Don't try to keep the entire presentation within the boundaries of the screen – and don't tune it for a precise window size. Inevitably, the resolution of your projector won't be the resolution you expected. In presentation maps, moreover, contrast is a good idea; projectors sometimes have fanciful color profiles, and room lights can easily wash out subtle color distinctions.

Remember that you don't need to describe every box and picture in your presentation map. It's usually more effective to pick out some particularly interesting notes to discuss in detail, allowing other notes to speak for themselves. People read much more rapidly than you can speak; giving your colleagues plenty of information ensures that they can use their time to best effect. Remember, too, that you're free to move around in the Tinderbox map; you can adapt your presentation on the fly, to respond to challenges and to accommodate your audience's immediate interests.

16. Information Farming

Information Farming[4]

Three fundamentally different and incompatible metaphors shape both the design of hypertext systems like Tinderbox and the way these designs are usually discussed and marketed.

Information Mining views pertinent information as a valuable resource to be efficiently extracted and refined. Successful mining tools are those which can most quickly extract valuable nuggets of precious fact from large repositories of base data. The classic measures of successful mining are recall, precision, and cost.

Information Manufacturing views the acquisition, refinement, assembly and maintenance of information as a continuous enterprise, employing teams of specialists to implement acquisition procedures and management strategies. In contrast to mining, with its individualistic emphasis on seizing information and opportunity, the rhetoric of the information factory values continuity of process over individual entrepreneurship. Successful information factory tools are those which create stocks of corporate information through inexpensive, interchangeable labor. The classic measure of successful factory systems is usability: ease of initial training, productivity, and accuracy of work product.

Portions of this chapter originally appeared, in somewhat different form, in "Enactment in Information Farming", *Proceedings of Hypertext '93*, ACM, Baltimore. © 1993 by the Association for Computing Machinery.

Information farming (or information gardening) views the cultivation of information as a continuing and frequently collaborative activity performed by people working to achieve changing individual and common goals. Where the mine and factory serve the organization, the information farm is a computational space where colleagues and employees may work together on shared tasks and also pursue individual goals. The focus is neither on extraction (as in the mine) nor on stockpiling (as in the information factory), but on continuous cultivation and community.

The vision of information farming is integral to the romantic school of hypertext, and the different goals of the information farm and information mine have been a fertile source of misunderstanding between the hypertext and information-retrieval communities.

The design goals of farm tools differ from the goals we usually apply to mining tools and factory systems. Because farming is a continuous activity, measures of discrete transactions (e.g. recall rates) are less central to farming than to mining. Moreover, traditional human-computer interface studies concentrate on easily measured, everyday phenomena – the repetitive activities of the factory rather than the disparate activities of the information farm. The success of farming systems lies at least as much in the extent to which they can convey insight or explain extraordinarily difficult concepts as in their facility for expressing routine matters. Anecdotes and reading logs – records of personal experience over an extended course of thoughtful use and introspection – are a more characteristic approach to studying actual information farms and farmers than statistical surveys of sample subjects.

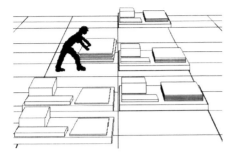

Figure 54. A user's avatar, seen at work sorting the messy piles and spatial aggregates found in the fields of an information farm.

The Challenge of Research Notes

The essence of research is discovery, and therefore uncertainty. We don't know the answers to the questions we are posing. We generally don't know, in advance, precisely how we will find the answers. In the course of research, we may redefine the questions we set out to explore, and will almost certainly discover unexpected avenues of inquiry and unanticipated relationships.

A bureaucrat or administrator may be able to carry out a project by following a familiar procedure, by filling out appropriate forms or composing suitable reports. Though the procedure may require skill and expertise, and though the outcome might be uncertain, the steps to be followed and the methods employed will be determined by the nature of the task. If we are setting out to pass a new law, we can anticipate the need for drafting the legislation, for subcommittee hearings, for committee approval and negotiations with Congressional or parliamentary leadership. Negotiations with individual legislators will doubtless be needed, as well as press conferences and constituent briefings. A floor debate will need to be managed, and executive assent secured. Achieving all this may be a challenge and the outcome might be uncertain, but the nature of the process is likely to fit our expectations rather closely.

Research, on the other hand, leads us in unexpected and unpredictable directions. We may begin seeking answers to one question, and then discover that those answers depend on additional questions which we don't fully understand. Some of those questions, in turn, may require new expertise. We may need to consult other researchers, or to locate new sources of information, or to construct instruments capable of performing measurements we require.

That this uncertainty is characteristic of scholarship and scientific research is proverbial, but the same uncertainty pervades business research of all kinds, from lab research and product development to market research, procurement, and competitive intelligence. We set off to determine the best price for a new product, and before long we find ourselves searching through historical precedents (has anything like our radical new proposal been tried before?), focus groups, customer interviews, microeconomic theory, and governmental regulation. We set out to reduce the number of accidents on the shop floor, and before we're done we find ourselves learning to run a numerical milling machine, reviewing new medical studies on occupational health, constructing models of new part-management stockpiles, negotiating with unions, and interviewing design experts on color theory and lighting.

We can't plan our research notes in advance, because we don't know what shape they will take. And we can't profitably commence our research without an efficient way to record notes.

On Premature Commitment

Fear of premature commitment – of making poor initial choices in our project that will ultimately lead us astray – can lead to paralysis and inertia. We gather a fact and want to record it; where do we put it? If we misclassify the fact, it might be lost or misinterpreted. The early classification error might be discovered later, to our surprise and embarrassment. It is tempting, then, to put off any kind of classification until the conclusion is evident, to wait until we can foresee the result. In the worst case, we may find ourselves choosing the result toward which our "research" will aim, converting our inquiry into mere polemic.

Premature commitment is most problematic when reorganization is difficult. Databases, for example, generally require that the structure of tables and records and fields be determined before the database is populated. Redesigning the database is possible, to be sure, but architectural changes are onerous and time-consuming. If the data are not well chosen at the outset, a great deal of data entry may need to be repeated, or complex and error-prone conversion tools will need to be implemented.

Outliners, similarly, excel when the overall structure of the problem is evident from the outset. If we already know our argument and simply wish to amass and organize evidence, then an outline can be an effective tool. If our path is less clear, however, the utility of an early outline is doubtful. How shall we choose the top-level categories, for example, when we don't yet know what issues we may need to consider? When seemingly major questions may turn out to be largely irrelevant, and when completely unforeseen issues may later emerge as critical questions, our preliminary outline may soon turn out to be very far from corresponding to our conception of the problem. As the outline diverges from our comprehension, its ability to aid us diminishes; eventually, we may find ourselves treating it as a long list of disordered text items that we access primarily by searching.

Let's take a practical and familiar research problem, one that is open-ended (as most good problems are) and yet sufficiently familiar and concrete that we can readily grasp the issues involved.

Travel Notes

Let us examine the research needs that underlie an individual's comprehensive, personal, and long-term plan of travel.

Many professionals travel routinely. Some move chiefly in one region, others travel chiefly between a few destinations. In addition to routine travel, it's likely that extraordinary destinations will be suggested from time to time. Occasional conferences and trade shows help one to keep in touch with the field and with colleagues. Vacations afford relaxation or excitement, a chance to learn or a chance to exercise unused skills. Family events often take us to new places. So, too, do business opportunities and crises.

It is possible, to be sure, to forgo planning – to go where the job sends you and to relax where your family prefers. But knowing in advance where we might go and what we might do affords a variety of attractive benefits:

- We may be able to take advantage of proximity. If a conference is scheduled in London, we might conveniently visit customers in the City, or colleagues from Oxford or the Royal College of Art, or old college friends who now live in Kent.
- We may also be able to anticipate needs in order to optimize opportunities. Perhaps we know that we need to visit Aunt Mary in Oshkosh sometime. When is Oshkosh likely to be most interesting to us, and our visit most convenient for Aunt Mary? Perhaps we can foresee a need to visit our client's new factory near Paris: with six months' notice, we can learn a little French and learn a little about or client's firm, while if we wait for the boss to hand us the tickets we'll have no choice but to spend the plane flight reviewing our files and wishing we knew what was missing.
- We may also be able to anticipate problems and accommodate mishaps by planning for them. What must we pack? What documentation needs to accompany us? How do we reach our contacts? Whom do we see if our contact is unavailable? Sooner or later, travel is bound to lead to confusion and chaos; by anticipating possible failures and by recording your plans, your alternative plans, and your constraints, you'll be better able to improvise in the face of uncertainty.

Notes about travel plans are a fascinating notetaking problem. Travel notes have four important purposes:

- **Planning**. Perhaps I know that I will arrive at Heathrow late and depart early the next day. I ought to eat. London is a great metropolis; why waste a night if I can spend it to good effect?

- **Doing**. It's always good to know what your plans were, because they're bound to change. Having a detailed plan is convenient, but being able to drill down to find the plans you'd considered and rejected can be vital when your schedule comes unglued, or when an unexpected opportunity comes along.
- **Telling**. Sharing stuff you know is now easy, and it creates a casual web of knowledge. Esther Dyson has long been one of the best tech journalists around; she famously knows more about hotel swimming pools around the world than just about anyone, because she travels a lot and cares about swimming pools. Because she publishes an industry newsletter, she has been able to share this knowledge with her customers at little or no cost. It used to be hard to share information like this; the casual web makes it easy.
- **Returning**. You might pass this way again; you need to remember where it was that you had those wonderful muffins. After trying a tasty dish, I'll often say, "I'm going to make this!", and then I often forget to try.

You've got to write it down, because you're going to need it.

Let's start a series of notes about travel notes. We begin by making a new Tinderbox document and adding these notes about why travel notes matter. For good measure, I'll also drag into it some of the email I received about dining at Heathrow. I'll drop a distinctive color scheme on the document as well, so I'll know when I'm working on my travel notes.

Making Spaces

When starting a new project, some people dive in and add lots of data. Others like to build the perfect structure first, with plenty of apparatus and automation. We'll begin, instead, by sketching out some very preliminary ideas, using adornments to set aside space for some notes we want to take.

The   adornments   on   the   left   side   of

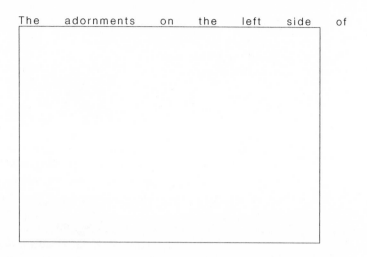

Figure 55 are meta spaces – notes about these notes. I've got a meta space for features I want to add, and another one for topics I want to discuss, and yet another area for observations about the project. A fourth meta space will hold some prototypes.

The remaining adornments represent places. Some of these are trips I've planned; those have a thin violet border and white titles. Others represent trips I'm thinking about – travel I expect I'll need to undertake, trips I'd like to plan if I can find the time. These tentative trips have a thicker, lighter border and blue titles.

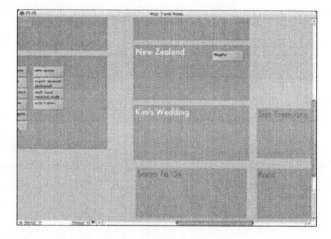

Figure 55. Pouring data into travel notes. We begin by adding adornments to help organize notes about upcoming trips.

Adornments are a *lightweight organizers*. They organize space and describe intentions, but they represent a very slight commitment. Not sure where something fits? You can place it at the edge of an adornment, or just outside an adornment, or astride two adornments.

This is an example of spatial hypertext – using proximity to represent a weak connection. It's also an example of the limitations of outliners: if you don't know how things need to be organized, you can't get started with the organization.

It's possible we'll revise this scheme, and revamp the map according to date. Or we might organize by region instead of place. Some other organizing principle might emerge. **I don't know what I'm doing yet:** the principle of least commitment advises me to sketch a simple and easily changed organizing system and get on with the work.

We could be even simpler: why organize at all? I might try to rely completely on search. That's the idea behind One Big Text File, and also the idea behind similarity-seeking tools. I want **some** organization because it helps remind me what I want to think about: for example, it's good to start thinking about travel you'd *like* to undertake as well as travel your business and family *require*. If you know what you'd like, you can work for it: you don't want to wake up and realize you never saw the Pyramids because you didn't have an urgent business reason for going.

Write It Down

Before we get much further with the Travel Planning Notes structure, it's time to go ahead and make notes. **It's sometimes tempting to make elaborately automated documents when you ought to be simply making some notes.** Don't get tied up in infrastructure: go ahead and start making notes. Write it down.

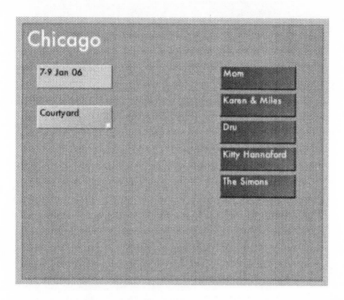

What should we note down? Everything we don't want to forget! The (proposed) dates for the trip. The people I'm hoping to see. Places I'd like to visit. Things I want to do. Things I *need* to get done.

I've started a simple color coding scheme here. Red things are people. Green things are dates. I don't *know* this will be useful, at this point, but it helps focus my thinking and suggests new ways to organize and analyze.

It's usually preferable to make lots of small notes instead of a few long ones. Small notes are easier to locate. Because they are tightly focused, small notes make more sense as link destinations. By sticking to one point, short notes are easier to update when things change; if someone is going to be in Hong Kong when I'm in Chicago, I can move them to the next Chicago trip.

Continuous Incremental Advantage

The key to success in a project like these travel planning notes is **continuous incremental advantage**. Each bit of work spent on the project needs to make your work better – faster, smoother, more accurate, more creative, less stressful.

We've only just started building travel notes, but already they're better than the best we'd expect from other technologies.

- **Trying to remember** it all is the reason we got started on this in the first place. You can't do it. (If you can do it, and it doesn't cause you stress, you're probably not reading this topic.)
- **Using lots of little bits of paper** is a non-starter. The yellow stickies and backs of envelopes and legal pads cause clutter, and they don't really help you find what you need.
- **One Big Text File** is probably the most competitive technology. We've got all the key advantages of One Big Text File in Tinderbox – ease of adding information, fast search for finding things, easy printing when you need a note on paper. But we've also got spatial hypertext for brainstorming, color coding, and links – and we're just getting started.
- **Databases** have a big impedance mismatch; we need to design the data model (and get the right data model) before we can even begin populating the database. With a database, we'd still be getting started.
- **Outliners** share some of the problems with databases and have most of the limitations of one big text file. We need to know how to organize the file right away. We can't know this yet. So we end up dithering, or we end up with One Big Text File in an outliner.

Some subtle knowledge representation issues might perplex us at first, but can be accommodated with relative ease. What if your mom lives in Fargo in the summer, but always spends the winter in Dallas with Aunt Jane? Easy enough in Tinderbox: make an *alias,* drag it to Dallas, and put it right next to Aunt Jane.

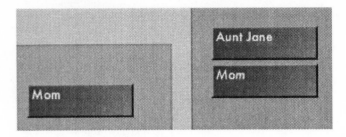

Thanks to aliases – shown here by italics – the same note (not a copy) can be in two places.

Smart Adornments

In our Travel Planning Notes, I've made some prototypes for People, Lodging, Food, Museums, and trip Dates. All these prototypes are gathered together in one corner of the document, which makes them easy to find and which serves as a handy legend to help us (or our assistants) remember that those notes with the gold borders are hotel reservations.

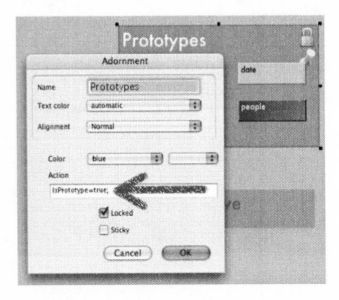

We can customize Tinderbox in a few seconds to make this legend even smarter. We simply add an action to the adornment underneath the prototypes: **IsPrototype=true;** Now, any note we create here will automatically be set up to be a prototype. Tinderbox "knows" you're using this part of the map to collect prototypes, and recognizes that if you add a new note here, you're probably intending for it to be a prototype.

We didn't expect, when we designed Tinderbox, that you'd use adornments to do this. We didn't expect, for that matter, that this is something you'd want to do. **You don't have to send us a feature request**, and you don't have to hire anyone to do custom programming. Just do it, and you're done. Change your mind? You can modify the action, or remove it, just as quickly.

A benefit of Tinderbox's simple and regular data structure – everything is an attribute – is that you can easily add semantics and behavior to your documents.

Travel Notes: Making a List

We've been talking a lot about long-range planning. Let's look at improving some short-range matters: making sure we bring what we need on each trip, without wasted time or unnecessary anxiety. What we need, of course, is a **packing list**.

To begin, I make a BIG list of everything I might want to take along on the kinds of trips I usually take. This is the **prototype** packing list, and it's just a typical prototype.

Now, when I want to plan what should be packed for a specific trip, I just make a new packing list, based on the prototype. It starts out with the same text as the prototype list – everything I'm likely to need.

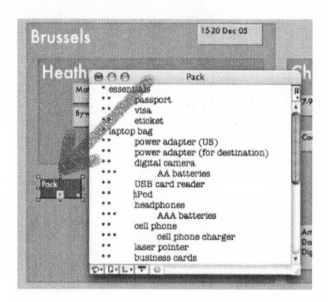

For each trip, I create a fresh instance of the packing list, based on the Packing List prototype. It starts out by listing every item on the generic packing list. I won't need every item on every trip, of course. I can quickly delete the items I don't want to pack, and add the specific items I'll want to bring only on this trip.

As I revise the list, I may discover things I want to add to the prototype packing list, so they'll be on the next packing list I make. That only takes a moment. It's another example of **incremental formalization** in Tinderbox; I don't have to worry about getting the prototype exactly right, because I can always change it later.

What could be easier? I just double-click on the trip, tell Tinderbox I want a packing list, and I'm all set.

Because I'm feeling lazy today, I add a rule to the packing list prototype:

```
if(Name=untitled){Name="pack list";Width=2;}
```

Now, I don't even need to name the packing lists – Tinderbox will name it automatically. If I do give the packing list a name – if, for example, I make separate packing lists for Linda and for me – Tinderbox respects the name I chose.

Checking It Twice

It's great to have a good packing list, but it's important to check the list. You've got to write things down, but sometimes you also need to read them again.

Of course, we could instantly **print** the packing list. But that list is formatted for the screen; if we start printing it, we'll be tempted to make it look better on the page.

If we want it to look good on the page, a nice approach turns out to be **HTML Export**. That's right – we export the packing list to HTML, even though we have no intention of putting it on the Web. HTML is a good text format, and CSS stylesheets give us good control over how our lists look on the page. Set up some simple templates, press preview, and here's what we get in Safari.

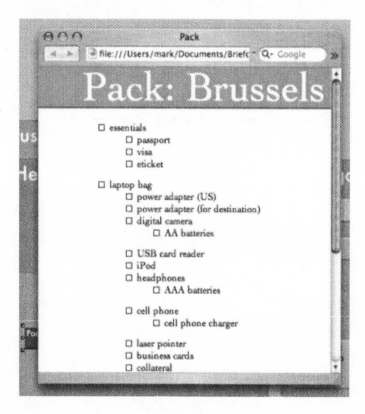

I confess I got a little carried away here, and wasted about 45 minutes tinkering with styles to get it just right. A little extra space between categories, a nice header, flexible scaling in case I need a wallet-size version of the checklist. Your mileage will vary (and you can probably make it look good in much less time).

Using Agents

Tinderbox agents can be useful for complex and sophisticated tasks, but some of the most useful agents can be set up in seconds.

You'll recall that we created a few prototypes to represent different kinds of notes – notes about people, notes about dates, notes about packing. For example, for trips that are already scheduled, I always have at least one note giving the dates of the trip. Unscheduled treks, such as notes about places I want to go but for which I have no immediate plans, don't have any Date notes.

I can easily set up an agent to gather all these Date notes in one list.

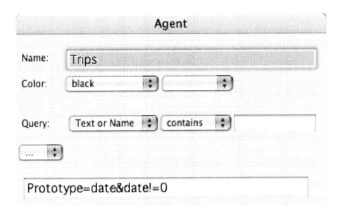

While I'm at it, I can have the agent sort the notes by date, too. Instantly, I've got a high-level itinerary.

17. Planning with Tinderbox

Your calendar is a calendar

Many Tinderbox users are also drawn to PDAs and electronic organizers. Almost all PDAs offer ToDo lists and memo programs of various degrees of sophistication. But often, initial enthusiasm yields to frustration, and the excitement of a new, sophisticated palmtop too often turns to unease and resentment.

PDAs are superb at managing time and contacts. They always know what time it is. They never forget. They're easy to use. In fact, success with a PDA really depends on two simple factors:

- You need to have the PDA with you, always. If you leave it behind, you'll have to write appointments on scraps of paper. Or, worse, you may simply try to remember them. Either way, you'll eventually find that some appointments aren't in your PDA.
- You must look at your PDA from time to time. If you never glance at your calendar, it cannot help you. But using your PDA for ToDo lists gradually encumbers that device with a host of tasks you once intended to do, but didn't get round to doing. All ToDo lists become, in time, tinged with guilt, for who among us has time and opportunity to accomplish everything we'd like (or ought) to undertake?

If you mix your ToDo list and your scheduler, sooner or later you'll leave it in your pocket because you just don't want to be reminded *again* that you ought to buy a gift for your niece. Because you don't want to check your ToDo list, you'll forget things that you really want to do. Eventually, you'll forget appointments.

Once you can't trust your scheduler, its value diminishes rapidly. The solution is simple: use your calendar exclusively for things that need to be done on specific days, at specific times.

Theater tickets and press conferences are tied to specific dates and times; if you aren't in the right place at the right time, you've missed the boat. Most business tasks give us more flexibility. We can defer a task in order to address a more critical need. We can delegate a task to a colleague. We can sometimes arrange for a contractor or other outside organization to perform the task for us. We might redefine the scope or the schedule of a task to meet changing business needs or to leverage new capabilities.

Planning for Change

Once we have reserved the calendar for tracking *events* – things that happen at specific dates and times – we're free to use Tinderbox for the more complex and volatile task of planning what needs to be done, and deciding who should be doing it.

Planning is an ongoing activity. You can't simply draw up a plan, announce it, and expect your team to execute it. Sooner or later, unforeseen factors and unexpected delays will change the plan. Priorities will change, making some minor tasks critical and rendering other tasks irrelevant. Team members will depart for other jobs. New staff will arrive to lend a hand.

Let's suppose, for example, that we've been tasked to manage our company's Advanced Widget Program. A year from now, we want to announce a new, high-performance widget, a fresh design that will bring new technology and fresh marketing ideas to build upon our current, successful Widget. Eighteen months from now, these Advanced Widgets need to be shipping to customers – and giving the company stronger margins.

You've built a team of experienced leaders from the key departments, and you've scheduled weekly planning meetings to give everyone a chance to report on their progress and to raise concerns.

Tinderbox On The Wall

The Tinderbox map makes an effective meeting aid. Simply plug your laptop into a projector, open the map to fill the screen, and you've got a malleable visual aid to focus your discussions. Because Tinderbox lets us create (and share) a persistent, intelligent, and flexible document, Tinderbox can do things to which no drawing program or whiteboard can aspire.

We might begin, simply enough, by adding a few adornments to suggest one possible way to organize our plans.

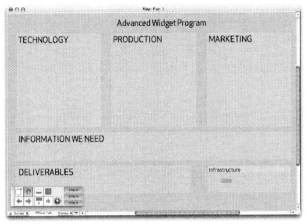

Figure 56. We can quickly sketch the framework of a planning document, perhaps a few minutes before the first team meeting.

Adornments set aside parts of the window for different purposes. These are just an initial guess; the adornments will change, expand, and shift many times over the coming weeks and months.

Notice, too, that these adornments aren't a taxonomy or a class system; they're just guidelines. Early in the first meeting, for example, the discussion turns to manufacturing: could new technology facilitate more automation on the production floor? It's a good question, possibly the key to meeting our target of improved margins. But where does the task fit? In the map view, we can let it straddle two or even three areas.

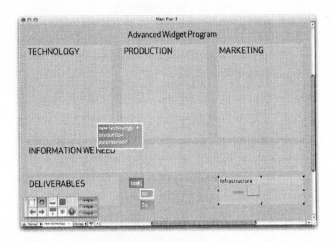

Figure 57. At the outset, it's apparent that we need to investigate new technology and its impact on production. The task doesn't fit neatly into any of our categories, but it's easy enough to situate it informally in the map.

In the bottom-center of Figure 57, we've also added a few small notes that serve as a legend or visual key. They remind us, for example, that Bill's tasks have a thick white border.

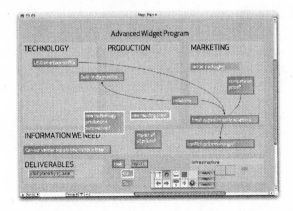

Figure 58. As the meeting progresses, we add more tasks. We can begin to make assignments and set priorities, as well as identifying relations among tasks.

In the course of the meeting, we'll be able to identify a wide variety of tasks. Some will be urgent, others can be deferred for a while. Some tasks, while not urgent, might usefully be done early in the project. Others might be left until later, or perhaps postponed entirely. Since the map is large (and we can always make it larger), there's no harm in recording a task we might decide can wait.

Often, setting priorities amongst dozens or hundreds of tasks is a formidable and daunting undertaking. Is resolving our vendor supply question the 47th-most urgent task, or the 39th? Trying to assess priorities is much easier, however, within local clusters. For example, we might try to place top priority *above* tasks that seem less urgent. By adjusting positions when we notice opportunities, we can express relationships in which we feel confident without worrying too soon (or too much) about priorities we don't yet understand.

We can also add some user attributes that we're bound to require. **Who** identifies who is responsible for managing and reporting on the task. **When** is the task's expected completion date, while **Deadline** is the latest date to which the task can be allowed to slip. **Finished** can be checked when the task is done.

Agents can now begin to help us visualize data; for example, one agent inside **Infrastructure** looks for all Bill's tasks and gives them a broad white border.

> **Tip:** It can be tempting at this stage to embark on very elaborate schemes, with dozens of attributes and myriad agents. Remember, though, that people find it tedious to fill out long lists of metadata; if you ask your team members to add lots of metadata with each new task, they may avoid using the system at all.
>
> A maxim of the popular *Agile* school of development says, "You aren't going to need it!" At this early stage, with only a few tasks and deliverables in the map, you won't get much leverage from your elaborate automation. Try to keep the infrastructure simple, at first, while the map is small. As the map grows and the plans become more elaborate, you'll need more agents – but by then you'll have a better feel for which agents you really need.

18. Bibliography

1.   Allen, D., *Getting Things Done: The Art Of Stress-Free Productivity*. 2002, New York: Penguin.

2.   Bernstein, M., *The Bookmark and the Compass: Orientation Tools for Hypertext Users*. SIGOIS Journal, 1988. 9(1988): p. 34-45.

3.   Bernstein, M., M. Joyce, and D.B. Levine. *Contours of Constructive Hypertext*. in *European Conference on Hypermedia Technology*. 1992. Milano: Asssociation for Computing Machinery.

4.   Bolter, J.D., *Writing Space*. 1991: Lawrence Erlbaum Associates.

5.   Davis, H.C. *Referential Integrity of Links in Open Hypermedia Systems*. in *The Proceedings of the Ninth ACM Conference on Hypertext and Hypermedia, Hypertext 98*. 1998. Pittsburgh, PA: ACM.

6.   Garzotto, F., P. Paolini, and M. Bernstein, *Tools for Designing Hyperdocuments*, in *Hypertext/Hypermedia Handbook*, E. Berk and J. Devlin, Editors. 1991, McGraw-Hill: New York. p. 179-208.

7.   Glushko, R.J. *Design Issues for Multi-Document Hypertexts*. in *Hypertext'89*. 1989. Pittsburgh.

8.   Halasz, F.G., T. P.Moran, and R.H. Trigg. *NoteCards in a Nutshell*. in *CHI+GI Proceedings*. 1987: ACM.

9.   Joyce, M., *afternoon, a story*. 1990, Eastgate Systems, Inc.: Watertown, MA.

10.   Kolb, D., *Socrates in the Labyrinth: Hypertext, Argument, Philosophy*. 1994, Eastgate Systems, Inc.: Watertown, Massachusetts.

11.   Landauer, T.K., *The Trouble With Computers: Usefulness, Usability, and Productivity*. 1995, Cambridge: MIT Press.

12.   Landow, G.P., *Hypertext 3.0:Critical Theory and New Media in an Era of Globalization,*. 2006, Baltimore: Johns Hopkins Press.

13.   Landow, G.P., editor, *The Victorian Web*. 1987-present.

14.   Leuf, B. and W. Cunningham, *The Wiki Way: quick collaboration on the Web*. 2001, Reading, Massachusetts: Addison-Wesley.

15.   Marshall, C., et al., *Aquanet: A Hypertext Tool to Hold Your Knowledge in Place*, in *Hypertext '91*. 1991: San Antonio. p. 261-275.

16.   Marshall, C.C. and R.A. Rogers, *Two Years before the Mist: Experiences with Aquanet*, in *ECHT'92*. 1992, ACM Press: Milano. p. 53-62.

17.   McCloud, S., *Understanding Comics*. 1993: Kitchen Sink Press.

18.   Miles, A., *Cinematic Paradigms for Hypertext*. Continuum: Journal of Media & Cultural Studies, 1999. **13**(2): p. 217-225.

19.   Moulthrop, S. *Hypertext and 'the Hyperreal'*. in *Hypertext '89*. 1989. Pittsburgh: ACM.

20.   Moulthrop, S., *Victory Garden*. 1991, Eastgate Systems, Inc.: Watertown, MA.

21.   Nelson, T., *Literary Machines*. 1982, 1987: Mindscape Press.

22.   Shipman, F. and C.C. Marshall. *Formality Considered Harmful: Experience, emerging themes, and directions on the use of formal representations in interactive systems*. in *CSCW*. 1999.

23.   Taylor, P.G., *"Hypertext-based art education: Implications for liberatory learning in high school."* Doctoral Dissertation. 1999: Penn State University.

24.   Trigg, R.H. and M. Weiser, *TEXTNET: A Network-Based Approach to Text Handling*. ACM Transactions on Office Information Systems, 1986. 4(1): p. 1-23.

Index